The Abingdon Children's Sermon Library

Volume 3

The Abingdon Children's Sermon Library

Volume 3

Edited by
Brant D. Baker

Abingdon Press
Nashville

Library of Congress Cataloging-in-Publication Data

ISBN - 978-0-687-65152-8
ISSN application in process.

08 09 10 11 12 13 14 15 16 17—10 9 8 7 6 5 4 3 2 1
MANUFACTURED IN THE UNITED STATES OF AMERICA

Contents

Contents

Contents

Contents

Contents

Introduction

What makes a for a great children's sermon? Good planning and preparation are a given and are well within the leader's control, just as cute responses and serendipitous replies are outside of their control. But it is our continuing conviction that *learning by experience* is what makes for a great children's sermon. Not lecture, not question and answer, but action, activity, and physical involvement are the keys to great moments with children in worship.

What follows, then, are fifty-two new sermons that seek to engage children by putting them in the action. Movement and merriment, exploration and echoes, songs and skits are all found in this third volume of the *Abingdon Children's Sermon Library*.

But there is something more here as well. Because what makes for a *really great* children's sermon is congregational involvement. We're not talking about the tired debate of whether children's sermons are for the kids or for the adults. The answer to that one is: both, but in the right order—communicating with children first and then inviting adults to join in the fun.

LETTING EVERYONE PLAY

The truth is that kids like it when adults play along. It validates what they are doing in a way far more meaningful than passive assent. This has always been the case, but is so much more the case in our culture of virtual game play (such as video games), which largely means playing alone. For child and adult to engage in play for the pure, unbridled joy of it, is good medicine for both. Again, children's sermons are first and foremost for the children, and so we may not want to move too quickly or too often to congregational involvement, but doing so is still a worthwhile goal, especially when it seems natural to do so.

There are a handful of fairly simple ways to bring the congregation closer to the action:

- **Move into their space.** Taking the children out into the sanctuary is a simple way to get them moving and also engage the congregation. There's plenty to explore in the average sanctuary, and along the way you never know who you'll bump into! (See "Take a Walk," p. 71.)

- **Readers/Singers.** The congregation can sometimes provide the background needed for a children's sermon. In "Four Stations of the Font" (p. 37), I invited the congregation to read four Bible verses as the children and I enacted each one. In "Doxology" (p. 97), Jeff L. Hutcheson turns the congregation into a choir to help end a sermon on living a life of praise. Anytime children are asked to sing as part of the sermon it will strengthen and encourage them to have the congregation singing along as well (see also "Reasons to Celebrate!" p. 60).

- **Vocal Echoes.** Bob Sharman has contributed several sermons to this volume that begin with the children echoing the key Bible verse for the sermon. While he hasn't specified that the congregation participate in this echo, it would be a simple matter to have the children echo the verse once and then invite the congregation to be part of the echo the second time. In his sermon, "Who Are the Children of God?" Bob extends the echo idea even further and assigns the congregation a key part late in the sermon, thus involving them even further (see p. 17).

- **Motion Echoes.** An obvious extension of the vocal echo is to echo any motions that the children may be doing. It isn't uncommon for me to teach motions to the children and then say something like, "Do you think we should ask the congregation to play with us too?" or "Let's ask the congregation to help us with this." It's always fun to see how eagerly the adults join in!

- **Props.** One of my favorite mechanisms for involving the congregation is to have them become props. Need a grove of trees for a sermon on Jesus' prayer at the Mount of Olives? No problem! Need some rocks to cry out during

Jesus' triumphal entry? It's covered! One of my favorite sermons using the congregation as props included some sneaky instructions that caused the landscape to suddenly change! (See "Walking In The Way," p. 73.)

• **Sound Effects.** Asking the congregation to provide sound effects is an extension of the props idea. Wind, earthquakes, large crowds of murmuring Israelites are all at the leader's fingertips! (See "When Things Get Bumpy," p. 46).

WHAT'S NEW!

In addition to all this great fun and the usual collection of both seasonal and ordinary time selections, this volume of the *Childrens' Sermon Library* has two engaging series. The first is a collection of three sermons, starting on page 69, that plays on the theme of taking a walk or hike ("Walking in the Truth," "Take a Walk," and "Walking in the Way"). The creative and energetic leader might want to get outfitted with boots and backpack to further enhance this midsummer fun.

The second series takes in the four Sundays of Advent as well as Christmas and Epiphany, and uses a clever device that plays off of Bethlehem as the "house of bread." See the "Bethlehem Bakery" series, which begins on p. 101.

I hope you and the congregation you serve will enjoy these series and all of the other good work that follows. May you be blessed in your ministry, especially as you welcome the little ones and bring joy to all of God's children.

Brant D. Baker

All Through the Year

Scripture: Psalm 105:8 (CEV)

Season/Sunday: The Sunday just after January 1

Focus: As we begin a new year, we believe that God will keep his promise to watch over us every day.

Experience: Children will see a new calendar to get a glimpse of all the days ahead. Then in honor of a special day in the year, their birthday, the children and the congregation will stand when they hear the month of their birthday called out.

Arrangements: You will need a calendar or date book for the new year.

Leader:	Good morning! I hope you all had a very merry Christmas. Now it's time to begin a brand new year. Can you tell me what new year we are beginning?
Children:	*(Children say the number of the new year.)*
L:	God has given us a brand new year! Let's say a prayer of thanksgiving—let's say "Thank you Lord for _year_."
Children:	"Thank you Lord for _year_."
L:	Let's try that one more time and ask the congregation to join us.
Children and Congregation:	"Thank you Lord for _year_."
L:	*(Hold up the calendar.)* In honor of _(year)_ I have a brand new calendar. Look at all those blank pages *(turn some of the pages so the children can see)*. See all those days coming up in the new year? That's a lot of days that add up to how many months?
C:	Twelve.
L:	Let's play a game in honor of all of the days and the twelve months in the new year. When you hear your

birthday month, I want everyone in the whole church who is born in that month to stand up and cheer. After we see who you are, you may sit back down again. (*Call out the months, allowing time for those with birthdays in that month to stand up and cheer.*) Birthdays are important days and it's fun to look for our birthday on the calendar. But there are other important days in the year, too. Can you name some of them?

C: The first day of school. Easter. The first day of summer vacation.

L: And there are sometimes bad or sad days. Can you tell me what might be a sad day?

C: A day when a pet dies. A day when a Grandma is sick. A day when I have a fight with my friend.

L: And there are regular old days too. Days when we go to school and to work. Days when we eat breakfast and take spelling tests and go to soccer practice. And you know what? On every single one of those days, God will be with us. There is a verse in the Bible that says, "[God] will never forget his agreement or his promises, not in thousands of years" (Psalm 105:8 CEV). That means that all through this year, and through all the years to come, God promises to watch over our lives. And that's a wonderful promise. In honor of God's promise to us, let's all stand up once more and have a prayer thanking God for this new year and the promise to watch over us . . . *(prayer).*

Barbara Younger

Sensing the Word of God

Scripture: Matthew 26:26-28 (KJV)

Season/Sunday: Lord's Supper

Focus: The word of God comes to us in many forms. The Lord's Supper is one of those forms, but is unique in its communication to us through our physical selves.

Experience: To become aware that we receive God's word in various ways, and to experience that word with the full variety of our senses.

Arrangements: You will need: a Bible and a picture or other visual representation of the bread (wheat) and wine (grapes), e.g. a stained glass window or wood carving on the front of a table. Presumably this sermon will be used on a day when Communion is being celebrated, so the communion table will be spread.

Leader:	Hello everybody, good to see you today. I'd like to read to you, "Jesus said, 'Take, eat; this is my body . . . Drink ye all of it; For this is my blood of the new testament.'" (Matt. 26:26-28). What did we do just now?
Children:	*(A certain guilty silence!)* Read the Bible?
L:	Well, I read the Bible. What did you do *(point to ear if the children need an added prompt)*?
C:	Listened?
L:	Listened, that's right! You heard the word of God. Ok, let's go over there *(move to visual representation of elements)*. Look up there. What's that a picture of?
C:	A cup. Some grapes. Wheat.
L:	Right, and what are we doing right now *(point at your eyes)*?

3

C: Looking?

L: Right! We're seeing the symbols for Communion. Great! Okay, everybody come with me up to the front. So far we've heard and we've seen. What's this *(point to Lord's Supper)*?

C: Food!

L: Food, and we call this food the Lord's Supper. Later on in the service what are we going to do?

C: Eat?

L: We're going to eat! God has given us so many ways to learn about God's word! We can hear the word of God, we can see the word of God, and we can eat— or taste—the word of God. And all these things are ways God has to remind us that God's word to us is that we are loved by God. Let's have a prayer and thank God for giving us all these ways to know of God's word and of God's love . . . *(prayer)*.

Brant D. Baker

Doing the Word of God

Scripture: James 1:22

Season/Sunday: Any

Focus: To distinguish between hearing God's word and doing God's word.

Experience: To experience helping someone in need, not only with our words but also our actions.

Arrangements: You will need several helpers. Select one person to be the person in need (PN). Also, arrange for two volunteers (V1 and V2) who will wear coats and hats, and who can memorize the brief dialogue below. Finally, invite one last person (V3) who can equip the children with a small blanket, a coat, some food, and a cup of water.

> **Leader:** Good morning boys and girls. *(As the children come forward the PN stands off to one side, shivering.)*
> **Children:** Good morning!
> **L:** *(Notice PN—"Sally.")* Look there's Sally. What is she doing?
> **C:** She looks cold. She is shaking.
> **L:** *(Two volunteers walk up dressed for winter.)* Hey, it's Bob and Jean.
> **V1:** Good morning. We were just out for a morning stroll. *(Noticing PN)* Boy, Sally looks cold.
> **V2:** Maybe we should go over and comfort her.
> **V1:** Yes, let's go comfort Sally. *(They walk over to Sally, who is still shivering.)* Be of good cheer Sally.
> **V2:** Yes, have a great day *(the volunteers walk away)*.
> **L:** Hmmm. Does Sally look comforted?

C: No, she is still shaky. She looks cold. They didn't do anything.

L: No, they didn't. They said some nice things, and that's important, but they didn't do anything to help her. The Bible says to be *doers* of the word, not just those who hear the word. What could they have done?

C: They could have given her a coat. They could have brought her a blanket.

L: Those are good ideas! Does anybody have any of those things?

V3: I do! I have a blanket, a coat, some food, and some water. Do you think these will help Sally?

C: Yes!

V3: Will you help me take them all to her?

C: Yes!

L: Let's go and help Sally, and we can even say some more comforting things to her as well. *(Pass out the supplies to the children. Then all walk over to Sally, where the children distribute items. Prompt them to say things like, "Jesus loves you and so do we," and "We're doing this in Jesus' name because we care for you.")*

L: That was great! Let's thank God for all the good gifts we are able to share with others . . . *(prayer)*.

Jeff L. Hutcheson

Jesus Listens

Scripture: Matthew 20:29-34

Sunday/Season: Any

Focus: The sermon invites the children to become followers of Jesus by identifying with the two blind men in the story.

Experience: The children will listen to a biblical account and repeat phrases as the story is told. The leader only needs a simple signal, such as a raised hand, to indicate the start and finish of the phrase the children are to repeat (indicated in bold print below). The congregation can be invited to participate as well, if desired.

Arrangements: None are needed except to have a copy of the script below.

Leader: Good morning! Today you're going to help me tell a story about Jesus. I'll say part of the story, but there is a part you need to say too, and you'll know that part because I'll raise my hand like this *(demonstrate hand signal)* so you know when your part starts and stops. But that's not all, you need to say your part in three different ways, first softly, then in a normal voice, and then loudly. Are you ready to give it a try?

Children: Yes!

L: Okay, here we go. One day as Jesus and his friends were leaving Jericho, the crowd said: **"Let's follow Jesus!"**

C: *(Whisper.)* "Let's follow Jesus!" *(Normal.)* "Let's follow Jesus!" *(Loud.)* "Let's follow Jesus!"

L: Two blind men sitting by the side of the road, pleaded: **"Jesus, have mercy on us!"**

C: *(Repeat phrase three times in three ways.)*

L: The crowd told the blind men: "**Be quiet!**"

C: *(Repeat phrase three times in three ways.)*

L: But the blind men shouted: "**Jesus, have mercy on us!**"

C: *(Repeat phrase three times in three ways.)*

L: Jesus stopped and listened to the blind men. He asked: "**What do you want me to do for you?**"

C: *(Repeat phrase three times in three ways.)*

L: The blind men answered: "**Jesus, let our eyes be opened.**"

C: *(Repeat phrase three times in three ways.)*

L: Jesus touched their eyes and the blind men exclaimed: "**We can see! Let's follow Jesus!**"

C: *(Repeat phrase three times in three ways.)*

L: That was great! Let's have a prayer and give thanks that we can see and follow Jesus too . . . *(prayer)*.

Phyllis Wezeman

Joyful Before God

Scripture: 2 Samuel 6:1-19

Season/Sunday: Any

Focus: This sermon explores the great joy experienced by King David and the people of Israel in the presence of the ark of God. The sermon links the story of joy to the joy within worship.

Experience: After hearing a description of the ark of God, the children will interact with the story via a listening game. When the children hear a *joy* word, they will place their hands over their hearts.

Arrangements: None are needed, unless you wish to show the ark's measurements with a tape measure.

Leader:	You look like great listeners! Have you ever heard a Bible story about an ark?
Children:	*(Will probably answer "Noah's ark.")*
L:	You're right! Noah did have a big boat called an ark, but today, I want to tell you about a different ark. This ark is called the ark of God or the Ark of the Covenant. It was a chest measuring 47 inches long, 27 inches wide and 27 inches tall. The holy chest was built of acacia wood and then completely covered over by a layer of real gold. All around the top of the chest was a special golden molding. The Israelites called it God's throne. Do you know what a throne is?
C:	A fancy chair for kings and queens.
L:	Yes! And God's throne was fancy too. Two carved cherubim with beautiful outstretched wings and angelic bowed heads stood on either side of the throne.

Just being near God's ark and throne brought such
joy to the people. Do you know what joy is?

C: Being really happy. Bubbles in your heart.

L: Yes, joy is a great feeling of happiness and delight.
Now, I'll tell you a joyful story about King David and
God's ark. Listen carefully, and when you hear a *joy*
word, touch your hand to your heart, like this
(demonstrate motion). Can you do it?

C: *(Repeat motion.)*

L: You might remember that David was the brave boy
who fought Goliath with his slingshot. Later, David
became a king who wanted to do great things. He decided to bring the ark of God to Jerusalem. King
David and the people of Israel went to the house of
Abinadab, where the ark rested. Soon, it was brought
outside. As the people came near the ark of God, they
were filled with **joy**.

C: *(Touch hands to hearts.)*

L: King David began dancing before God to show his
joy.

C: *(Touch hearts.)*

L: That day, they took the ark to the house of Obed-
edom, where it stayed for three months. While the ark
was there, good things happened for Obed's family, so
they were especially **joyful** to be near it.

C: *(Touch hearts.)*

L: Finally, King David was ready to take the ark to
Jerusalem. Once again, the people of Israel **rejoiced**
when the ark was brought near them.

C: *(Touch hearts.)*

L: Then he danced and danced and danced before God
with all his might. As he reached Jerusalem, the people were **overjoyed**.

C: *(Touch hearts.)*

L: The people shouted God's praises and **joyously** played
their trumpets.

C: *(Touch hearts.)*

L: King David brought the ark into a special tent and
worshiped God with many offerings. Filled with **joy**,
he blessed the people in the name of God.

C: *(Touch hearts.)*

L: Next, the king gave everyone bread, meat, and raisins to eat. The people celebrated with heartfelt **joy**. The ark was in Jerusalem at last!

C: *(Touch hearts.)*

L: And for us, it is a **joy** to be near God . . .

C: *(Touch hearts.)*

L: . . . in this house of worship. Here we sing praises, play music, pray, and hear the word of God. During our worship, we can open our hearts to God with **joy**.

C: *(Touch hearts.)*

L: Let's bow our heads for a prayer, using the words of a wonderful hymn. I'll say a few of the words, and then you repeat them. Ready?

> Joyful, joyful, we adore thee *(pause for echo)*,
> God of Glory, Lord of Love *(pause)*;
> hearts unfold like flowers before thee *(pause)*,
> opening to the sun above *(pause)*.
> Henry Van Dyke, 1907

Amen!

Lisa Flinn

Love One Another

Scripture: John 15:12

Season/Sunday: Valentine's Day

Focus: Jesus calls us to love one another.

Experience: Children will enjoy meeting a well-loved stuffed animal before a discussion about loving others.

Arrangements: Locate a much-loved and worn stuffed animal. If such an animal isn't part of your household, you can borrow one. This is a fun request to send out on your church e-mail loop: "Needed for children's sermon. Much-loved and worn stuffed animal." If you borrow an animal, be sure you know the animal's name and a few other tidbits. If you cannot locate a much-loved animal, bring a newer one. You can comment that in time, this animal will be worn with love. Demonstrate with a few hugs. You will also need to purchase inexpensive valentines or create homemade valentines for the children. Homemade valentines can be as simple as construction paper cut into the shape of hearts. Sign each valentine in a festive or silly way with the name of the stuffed animal friend.

Leader: *(Hold up the animal.)* What's this?
Children: *(Identify animal.)*
    L: But this is not just any old toy. This is *(say the animal's name, who the animal belongs to, and a few other tidbits.)* *(Name)* is very well loved. How can you tell?
    C: The fur is worn. Her dress is torn. His ear is missing.
    L: I brought *(Name)* today in honor of Valentine's Day. When I look at *(Name)*, I understand how much *(owner's name)* loves him or her. I'm glad that we

have toy animals for children to love, but I am even more glad that we all have people to love. Can you name someone you love?

C: My mom. Aunt Laura. My cousin.

L: Jesus commands us to love one another. Listen to this Bible verse: "This is my commandment, that you love one another as I have loved you" (John 15:12). Will you echo that with me? This is my commandment *(pause)*, that you love one another *(pause)*, as I have loved you *(pause)*.

Valentine's Day is a day when we especially celebrate love. Will you *(or "did you" if Valentine's Day has passed)* send any valentines this year?

C: I gave one to my teacher. We handed them out at our school party. I made one for my uncle who is in a nursing home.

L: Did you *(will you)* receive any valentines this year?

C: I got one from my grandpa. My cousin made me one. I will get some at my school party.

L: Those valentines celebrate loving one another. Guess who has a valentine for you right now? *(Hold the animal up even higher and nod its head.)*

C: *(Name)*!

L: Yes. In celebration of our love for one another, our friend *(Name)* has a valentine for each of you. Take the valentine home and keep it as a reminder that Jesus commands us to love one another. Before *(Name)* gives you your valentine, let's say a prayer celebrating love . . . *(prayer)*. *(Have the animal friend say goodbye to the children, or if your group is small, let each child give the animal a hug, kiss, or high five.)*

Barbara Younger

Thank You, God, for Feelings

Scripture: Psalm 35:1-3 (anger); Psalm 42:11 (sadness); Psalm 118:6 (fear); Psalm 147:1 (gladness)

Season/Sunday: Any

Focus: One of the challenges of growing up is dealing with emotions. Children will identify various feelings and thank God for the gift of emotions.

Experience: Children will make faces to show the emotions of children described in various life situations.

Arrangements: No special props are needed.

> **Leader:** Do you like to make silly faces? Show me your silliest face.
>
> **Children:** *(Make silly faces.)*
>
> **L:** Can you make faces that show feelings? Can your face show feeling scared? Angry? Sad? Happy?
>
> **C:** *(Make faces in response to each emotion named.)*
>
> **L:** God has given us all wonderful faces to show our feelings. Sometimes we call *feelings* our *emotions.* I'm going to tell some stories about emotions. When I finish telling the story, make a face that shows the feelings that go along with the story.
> The first story is about a girl named Julia. One night Julia was sleeping when the sounds of a thunderstorm woke her. She saw lightning outside her window. She heard thunder. Then, the lights went out in her house. Can you make a face to show me how Julia felt?
>
> **C:** *(Make a scared face.)*
>
> **L:** In our second story, a boy named Michael loved to play soccer. He practiced with his team every week,

and he was very excited about their first game. When the day of the game came, Michael heard raindrops on his bedroom window. Soon after, his coach called and said the game was cancelled because of the rain. Show me with your face how you think Michael feels.

C: *(Make a sad face.)*

L: Listen to our third story about a girl named Savannah. Savannah loved to paint pictures. She worked very hard to make her pictures beautiful. Whenever she painted, Savannah kept a small cup of water close by to clean her paintbrush. One day while Savannah was painting a picture, her little sister accidentally knocked over the cup of water and spilled it all over Savannah's painting. Make a face to show how Savannah might feel.

C: *(Make an angry face.)*

L: Our last story is about a boy named Ethan. Ethan's family had a special celebration for him on his birthday. His family took Ethan to his favorite restaurant for dinner. After dinner they ate cake and ice cream, and Ethan opened his presents. Can you make a face to show me how Ethan felt?

C: *(Make a happy face.)*

L: Listening to these stories brought up all kinds of emotions. Who gave us emotions to begin with?

C: God? Jesus?

L: That's right. In fact the Bible has a lot to say about emotions, especially in the Psalms, where we find out that it is okay to have emotions of fear and anger, sadness and gladness, and more. So, why do you suppose God gave us emotions?

C: *(Share their thoughts.)*

L: Those are all good ideas. It sure seems like emotions are useful. When we're scared, it's a warning that there may be danger. We may need to get help to be safe. When we feel sad or mad we know something around us is not right and needs to be changed. Glad feelings are God's gift to bring us happiness. God gives emotions for a reason. We shouldn't ignore them. When we have strong feelings like anger, fear, or sadness, we can talk to an adult we trust and talk to God. When we are happy, we can share that feeling with everyone around! Let's thank God for our feelings . . . *(prayer)*.

Heather Hagler

Who Are the Children of God?

Scripture: 1 John 3:1 (NIV)

Season/Sunday: Any

Focus: This sermon focuses on the biblical concept of the children of God.

Experience: Children will discover that we are all God's children, and will lead a short litany of proclamation for and with the congregation.

Arrangements: None needed

Leader: Good morning children of God. I want you to know that God says to call you children of God. Would you like to see where?

Children: Yes.

L: It is right here in 1 John 3:1, in fact, why don't you repeat it after me, "How great is the love" *(pause for echo)*, "the Father has lavished on us" *(pause)*, "that we should be called children of God" *(pause)*, "and that is what we are!" *(Pause.)*
So, you are the children of God. Are there any other children of God around here?

C: No. Yes. In the nursery.

L: That's right, there are some children of God in the nursery. But I mean right here. Are there any more children of God right here?

C: No. Maybe. Yes?

L: Well, this verse is saying that if God loves us, then we are all children of God. That is very good news, I want you to know. Let's do this *(lower your voice conspiratorially and address the children)*: let's tell the rest of the congregation that they are God's children too! Will you help me?

C: Yes!

L: Okay, when I say, "Who are the children of God?" you point to them and call out, "You are the children of God!" And the second time I ask, say, "We are the children of God!" Ready?

C: Yes!

L: Let's stand up. Who are the children of God?

C: You are the children of God!

L: Who are the children of God?

C: We are the children of God!

L: That was great! Let's do it a couple more times, but let's give the congregation a part. *(To the congregation)* After the children answer the question, you all say, "That is what we are!" Everybody ready? Who are the children of God?

C: You are the children of God!

Congregation: That is what we are!

L: Who are the children of God?

C: We are the children of God!

Congregation: That is what we are!

L: That was fantastic! Let's have a prayer and give thanks that we are all children of God . . . *(prayer)*.

Bob Sharman

What about Crosses?

Scripture: Galatians 6:14a (CEV)

Season/Sunday: Lent

Focus: To recognize why we use the symbol of the cross.

Experience: The children will examine various styles of crosses and look for cross symbols in the place of worship.

Arrangements: Locate crosses of various styles and spend some time in your place of worship, checking for the cross design in the architecture as well as the items you use in worship. Sometimes the room itself is in the form of a cross, and if so plan to lay on the floor to see it better! If you have banners (or other paraments) with a cross on them for other seasons, have them available. If you would like, purchase a cross for each child.

Leader: Good morning! I've brought some interesting things with me this morning. Can you tell me how they are alike and how they are different? *(Pass the crosses around for the children to examine. If a cross is fragile, ask an adult to help you show it to children individually.)*

Children: *(Varied responses.)*

L: Look around in our sanctuary/place of worship. Do you see any other crosses?

C: *(Varied responses.)*

L: *(Point out any crosses in your worship area including the architecture.)* Where else have you seen crosses?

C: *(Varied responses.)*

L: We have crosses in our churches and sometimes in our homes. We even use crosses in our jewelry sometimes. Many people have used crosses for many different reasons. Some of the Native American people used the cross to represent the four winds that brought them rain. The Chinese used the cross in a square to represent the earth. In Egypt they had a symbol called the enclosed sun cross that represented four rivers flowing from paradise. The early Christians did not use crosses as a symbol. It's believed that they began to be used hundreds of years ago, around the year 400! That's when the Roman ruler, Constantine, became a Christian and declared that all Romans would be Christian.

Remember in the Ten Commandments we are told not to worship images but only to worship God. The cross is not something that we worship, but something that we use to remind us of Jesus and how he died for us. He died on the cross for what he believed about God. Some churches will use a cross with a figure of Jesus on it, and other churches use only an empty cross. The empty cross reminds us that God didn't let Jesus stay dead but raised him from the dead.

There is a verse in the Bible that says, "But I will never brag about anything except the cross of our Lord Jesus Christ." This is found in a letter Paul wrote to the church in Galatia. *(If you have crosses for each of the children, give them to them now.)* Let's have a prayer thanking God for this reminder of Jesus and how important he is to us . . . *(prayer).*

Delia Halverson

Created in God's Image

Scripture: John 3:14-21

Season/Sunday: Lent

Focus: Living into the image of Jesus.

Experience: Children will share who people say they look and act like.

Arrangements: You may take volunteers or you may prearrange a child or youth and the parent(s) they resemble. Also give some thought to whom you might call on as "looking like God" on the inside.

Leader: Good morning! Have you ever heard people say that so-and-so looks like their mom or dad?
Children: Yes. No.
L: Well, this is "Emily" and this is Emily's mom and dad. Now, do you think Emily looks like her mom or her dad?
C: I think she looks like her dad. I do too.
L: Have any of you ever had someone say that you look like your mom or dad?
C: My friends say I look like my dad. I look like both of them.
L: But now that's on the outside. Sometimes we may look like someone on the outside but on the inside we think and act more like someone else. Emily do you act more like your mom or you dad?
Emily: It's both, but a lot of the time I use my hands when I talk and I talk like my mom.
L: When we read the Bible we hear it say that we are made in God's image, and that we are like God. What do you suppose that means?

C: *(Various answers.)*

L: Those are some good answers. And do you know what? We happen to have someone here who looks exactly like God! That's right, do you see that guy right there on the second row? That's what God looks like. Now I don't mean on the outside, but on the inside. I know that guy right there: he really cares about people, and he takes care of people all the time and is nice to them. When that guy takes care of people, then we see what God looks like. And do you see this lady over here? Wave, "Ms. Heidi." That's what God looks like. No, not on the outside, but Ms. Heidi has a beautiful spirit and she likes to share all she has with other people. When she does that, that's what God looks like. Do you see anyone else here who looks like God? If you do, point to them.

C: *(Point to various people.)*

L: Yup, I think you're right! Let's have a prayer and give thanks that when we look into one another's eyes we see what God looks like . . . *(prayer)*.

Karen Evans

Talking to God

Scripture: Luke 11:1-13

Season/Sunday: Although this sermon could be used during any season, it is especially appropriate during Lent when we focus on repentance and our relationship with God.

Focus: God is always accessible. We can talk to God at any time and in any place, and we don't need any fancy equipment.

Experience: The children will talk about their experiences using high-tech devices to talk to family and friends and think about the fact that they don't need technical devices to talk to God.

Arrangements: Have on hand some of the following to serve as conversation starters with the children: cell phone, laptop computer, webcam, and two cans tied together with a string.

> **Leader:** This morning, I want to spend some time talking about the things we use to talk to each other. First, I want to show you this device that some people in the congregation might remember playing with when they were young. What do I have here?
>
> **Children:** It's two cans tied together with a long string.
>
> **L:** What do you think we can do with this?
>
> **C:** I don't know. My grandma said she used to play with cans.
>
> **L:** You can use the cans to talk to each other as an old-fashioned phone. Try it. Somebody hold one can to their mouth and another person hold a can to their ear and pull it tight. What happens?
>
> **C:** Not much!
>
> **L:** Is this the way that we talk to each other today?
>
> **C:** NO!
>
> **L:** How do you talk to your family and friends? Maybe you use some of these things? What do I have here?

C: A cell phone!

L: That's right! Does anybody in your family use a cell phone?

C: Yes, my mom! My sister. My brother. My dad!

L: What's this? Does anyone in your family use something like this to talk to family and friends?

C: It's a laptop computer.

L: That's right! How can we talk over the computer?

C: E-mail. Instant messaging. Video clips.

L: Has anybody ever used one of these? A webcam?

C: No.

L: Sometimes if you have a relative across the country or far away, you might use a webcam to talk to them. That way you can see them too! Today in our lesson, Jesus is telling us about how we can talk to God. Do we need any of these things to talk to God?

C: NO!

L: That's right. We don't need cans tied together with string or high-tech devices like cell phones, computers, or webcams to talk to God. Jesus' disciples wanted to know how to communicate with God. What did he do to communicate with God?

C: He prayed!

L: That's right. Jesus talked directly to God and he taught his disciples to pray too! What was the prayer called that he taught them?

C: The Lord's Prayer.

L: Do you know that prayer? Let's join together and talk to God now. Let's invite the congregation to join us.

All: Our Father...

L: That was pretty easy, wasn't it? Jesus wants us to know that we can always communicate with God. God didn't want phones or e-mail or anything else to get in the way of us talking to God, so we can always reach God. Remember, when you need to talk to God all you have to do is start talking! Now that we know how easy it is to talk to God, let's share a prayer to thank God for always being there and listening to us . . . *(prayer)*.

Susan M. Lang

Remember Jesus' Suffering

Scripture: Matthew 27:27-31

Season/Sunday: Lent

Focus: Recognize that Jesus understands what it is like to be made fun of.

Experience: The children will have the opportunity to feel the prick of a thorn and watch you make a crown of thorns as they hear the story of Jesus' ridicule.

Arrangements: Cut thorny branches that are limber enough to bend and place them in a box to be concealed until you use them. Bring garden gloves and clippers to work with. Ask an adult to be the object of your ridicule and sit with you.

Leader: Good morning! Did you see "Mr. Smith's" hair today? I really don't like it. I think it's a silly looking hairstyle!

Adult: *(Pulling away from the leader.)* You made me feel bad! This is the best I can do, and you're making fun of my hair!

Leader: *(To children.)* Why do you suppose he's upset?

Children: *(Varied responses.)*

L: To tell the truth, I like his/her hairstyle fine, but I was only saying that to remind us that it does upset people when we say unkind things about them. Have you ever had someone say something unkind about you?

C: *(Varied responses.)*

L: Having unkind things said about you is called being ridiculed. Did you know that God understands how we feel, because Jesus had unkind things said about him? One of the times he was ridiculed was just before he died. *(Pull out the thorny branches and garden gloves and begin forming a crown from the*

branches as you tell the story.) Jesus and his disciples
had gone to Jerusalem, the special city that had the
large temple where they often went to worship God.
The rulers did not agree with all of the things that
Jesus was telling the people about how they should
act and how they should worship God. The people
who followed Jesus even called him king sometimes.
The religious leaders were afraid that Jesus and his
followers would take over their jobs, and so they had
him arrested and the ruler of the land said that Jesus
should be killed. When he was waiting to be killed,
the soldiers decided to pretend that he was a king to
ridicule him. They took his clothes off and put a pur-
ple robe on him, and put him in front of them like a
king. They even took some thorny vines, like these,
and twisted them to make a crown and put that on
his head. Then they put a stick in his hand that was
like a scepter a ruler would hold, and pretended to
bow down to him like they would do for a king. The
soldiers not only said unkind things about him, but
they also spit on him and used the stick to hit him on
the head. After they had done all of this, they took
the robe off and took him to a hill outside of town to
be killed. *(As you finish the crown of thorns, hold it
out for the children to touch and feel the prick of the
thorns. Remind them that the thorns are sharp.)*
C: *(Some will touch the thorns; others may elect not to.)*
L: How do you suppose Jesus felt when the solders were
acting this way toward him?
C: *(Various answers.)*
L: Although Jesus was hurt by the things that they were
doing and what they were saying about him, he did not
change his mind about what he believed. Before he died
he asked God to forgive those who were doing this to
him. Will you pray with me?

Our God, you know what it's like to have people say
unkind things. It hurts us and makes us sad. Help us to
remember that you love us even when others seem to be
mean to us. Help us to forgive them as Jesus did. Amen.

Delia Halverson

Blessed Is the One Who Comes

Scripture: Based on Luke 19:28-40

Season/Sunday: Palm Sunday

Focus: Jesus as the King who comes from God.

Experience: The children will experience what it was like to be in the crowd that hailed Jesus as King.

Arrangements: The children should be given small palm or jade branches to wave during their responses.

Leader: One Sunday, Jesus instructed some of his disciples to go borrow a donkey. When they found the donkey, the owner said, "What are you doing? Why are you untying my donkey?" The disciples replied as Jesus had instructed them: "Because the Lord Jesus needs to borrow it." And the owner let them take the donkey away. After his disciples threw a few coats on the donkey's back, Jesus sat on it and began to ride. And as he did, all the people around shouted out, "Blessed is the One who comes in the name of the Lord!" Can you hear them? What did they say?

L & Children: "Blessed is the One who comes in the name of the Lord!"

L: Jesus rode the donkey down the long hill from the Mount of Olives and into the valley below Jerusalem. And all the while the people shouted,

C: "Blessed is the One who comes in the name of the Lord!"

L: The people took off their coats and laid them in the path for the donkey to walk on, just like how people today roll out a red carpet for important visitors. And all the while the people shouted,

C: "Blessed is the One who comes in the name of the Lord!"

L: Next, many of the people cut palm branches from the trees and waved them in the air *(wave a palm branch and encourage the children to do the same)*, and they continued to shout,

C: "Blessed is the One who comes in the name of the Lord!"

L: Jesus rode the donkey up the hill and right into the city of Jerusalem, the great city of God's King. And all the while the people waved palm branches and shouted,

C: "Blessed is the One who comes in the name of the Lord!"

L: Some of the leaders were upset by all the noise and activity. But still the people waved palm branches and shouted,

C: "Blessed is the One who comes in the name of the Lord!"

L: "Even if these people were to be silent," Jesus said, "God could make the stones shout." But there was no worry about that because the people would not be silent. They continued to wave palm branches and shouted with all their might,

C: "Blessed is the One who comes in the name of the Lord!"

L: Let's have a prayer to the blessed One who comes . . . *(prayer)*.

Randy Hammer

The Emotions of Easter

Scripture: John 20:1-18

Season/Sunday: Easter

Focus: To explore the wide range of emotions surrounding Easter.

Experience: The children will participate by enacting movements suggested by the leader for the last word in each sentence. This method can be used with a wide number of stories and ensures that the Bible story is memorable and meaningful.

Arrangements: In addition to a copy of the script the leader will need to know the facial and physical expressions that are intended for use.

   Leader: Good morning! Who knows what special day this is?
   Children: Easter!
      L: That's right, and today you need to help me. I'll tell the story of Easter and stop on a word. Whatever word I stop on, you need to repeat, and then we'll all show that word using our faces and our bodies. You'll catch on, are you ready? Here we go! When Mary walked to the tomb on Sunday morning she was SAD.
      C: *(Repeat the last word and gesture SAD through face and body movements.)*
      L: When Mary saw that the stone had been rolled away from the tomb she was FEARFUL.
      C: *(Repeat the last word and gesture FEARFUL through face and body movements.)*
      L: When Mary ran to tell Peter and John the news she was CONFUSED.
      C: *(Repeat the last word and gesture CONFUSED through face and body movements.)*

L: When Mary told the disciples that someone had taken Jesus' body they were FRIGHTENED.

C: *(Repeat the last word and gesture FRIGHTENED through face and body movements.)*

L: When Peter and John ran to the tomb they were PUZZLED.

C: *(Repeat the last word and gesture PUZZLED through face and body movements.)*

L: When John looked inside the tomb he was STARTLED!

C: *(Repeat the last word and gesture STARTLED through face and body movements.)*

L: When Peter went inside the tomb he was SHOCKED!

C: *(Repeat the last word and gesture SHOCKED through face and body movements.)*

L: And when John walked into the tomb, he was SURPRISED!

C: *(Repeat the last word and gesture SURPRISED through face and body movements.)*

L: But when the disciples returned home they were GLOOMY.

C: *(Repeat the last word and gesture GLOOMY through face and body movements.)*

L: When Mary wept outside the tomb she was LONELY.

C: *(Repeat the last word and gesture LONELY through face and body movements.)*

L: When Mary saw two angels sitting inside the tomb she was AMAZED!

C: *(Repeat the last word and gesture AMAZED through face and body movements.)*

L: When the angels asked Mary why she was crying, she was SORROWFUL.

C: *(Repeat the last word and gesture SORROWFUL through face and body movements.)*

L: When Mary told the angels that someone had taken Jesus' body she was SCARED.

C: *(Repeat the last word and gesture SCARED through face and body movements.)*

L: When Mary turned and saw a man standing behind her she was STUNNED.

C: *(Repeat the last word and gesture STUNNED through face and body movements.)*

L: When the man asked Mary why she was crying she was UPSET.

C: *(Repeat the last word and gesture UPSET through face and body movements.)*

L: When Mary asked the man to tell her where they had taken Jesus' body she was FORLORN.

C: *(Repeat the last word and gesture FORLORN through face and body movements.)*

L: When Jesus called Mary by name she was HONORED.

C: *(Repeat the last word and gesture HONORED through face and body movements.)*

L: When Mary responded to Jesus with the word *teacher* she was DEVOTED.

C: *(Repeat the last word and gesture DEVOTED through face and body movements.)*

L: When Jesus told Mary to tell the others that he was alive she was JOYFUL.

C: *(Repeat the last word and gesture JOYFUL through face and body movements.)*

L: When Mary replied, "I have seen the Lord," she was ALIVE.

C: *(Repeat the last word and gesture ALIVE through face and body movements.)*

L: When Jesus' followers remembered God's great gift of salvation they were LOVED!

C: *(Repeat the last word and gesture LOVED through face and body movements.)*

L: That was great! Thanks for helping tell that wonderful story. Let's have a prayer and thank God that in Jesus, we are saved and loved as well . . . *(prayer).*

Phyllis Wezeman

Who Encourages Our Faith?

Scripture: Luke 24:13-35

Season/Sunday: Sunday after Easter

Focus: In this sermon the children will hear how Jesus encouraged the faith of the two followers on the road to Emmaus, then learn the ways their church family encourages them.

Experience: The children will hear a synopsis of the Emmaus story and then meet some of the people who work to strengthen their faith. In turn, each will come forward, holding an object that represents a way to encourage others, and then each will speak to the children.

Arrangements: You will need some volunteers, listed below, as well as the symbolic objects they will hold. As you recruit the encouragers, ask each to bring the object and say the suggested phrase. Explain that you will call them by name, following the story.

Encourager	Object	Phrase
Pastor	Bible	"I preach the word of God, found in the Bible, to strengthen and encourage your faith."
Teacher	Lesson book	"I guide you in understanding the Bible stories and teachings."
Youth Leader	Cross	"I lead you in fun and fellowship in the name of Jesus, who died on the cross."
Choir Member	Hymnal	"The choir encourages your spirit with music."

| Missions Chair | Hammer/soup ladle/ hanger/ other | "By serving others in need, need, we encourage their faith in God, as well as our own." |

You may choose to add someone who is significant to the children of your church, such as a puppeteer in a theater ministry or a camp director.

Leader: Good morning! Was yesterday a good day for a walk?

Children: Yes. No.

L: Did you walk anywhere yesterday? Where?

C: The park; school; nature trail; around the neighborhood.

L: Have you ever walked seven miles?

C: No!

L: Today, I'll share a story with you about two of Jesus' followers who walked seven miles from Jerusalem to Emmaus and then walked seven miles back the same day! These two followers were talking about all the terrible things that happened to their Lord, like his death on the cross. Soon, another traveler joined them. He asked them what they were talking about. The two turned to the traveler with such sad faces. Together, they told him how Jesus had suffered at the hands of the priests, the officials, the crowds, and the soldiers. They were deeply discouraged. The traveler listened. They were also sad that Jesus' tomb was found empty that morning. Their friends had seen angels who said Jesus was alive. The followers did not know what to think. They had hoped Jesus was the one whom God had sent to save Israel. Now they weren't sure. Right away the traveler began explaining that the true Messiah must suffer before going to glory. As he walked with the two, he taught them Scriptures and encouraged their faith. In all the time the traveler walked and talked with the two, they did not know who he was. Can you guess?

C: Jesus?

L: Yes. The traveler was Jesus! When the group reached Emmaus, the followers begged the traveler to have supper with them. As he sat at the table with the two, the traveler broke the bread, then blessed it. Suddenly, the two followers saw that the man was Jesus! And in that moment, Jesus disappeared! With great excitement and hope, the two hurried back to Jerusalem to encourage the others with the good news. Just as Jesus helped his followers to understand his message and believe, there are people in our church who find ways to encourage our faith. Do you want to know who they are?

C: Yes!

L: *(One by one, call upon your volunteers.)* Let's thank these wonderful, encouraging people! *(Applause)* Let's a have a prayer and give thanks for these wonderful encouragers . . . *(prayer).*

Lisa Flinn

What If I Mess Up?

Scripture: John 21:15-17

Sunday/Season: Any, but a Sunday soon after Easter might work well.

Focus: Through the life of Peter we learn about human failings and God's forgiveness. Children need to know that Jesus loves us and forgives us when we sin.

Experience: When the children hear various events in Peter's life, they will decide if he made good choices or bad choices.

Arrangements: You will need to have a Bible handy with the passage marked to read during the sermon.

Leader: Can you tell me the names of some of Jesus' friends, the disciples?

Children: *(Some of the older children may be able to name one or two.)*

L: One of the disciples we read about many times in the Bible is Peter. There are many stories in the Bible about him. When the Holy Spirit came to the believers, Peter became a strong speaker who carried the message of Jesus to many people. Now, usually when we think of someone who is in the Bible, and who was a disciple, we think they would always make good choices and be peaceful and truthful. But before the Holy Spirit came to the disciples, Peter didn't do any of these things! In fact, let me tell you a few stories about Peter. At the end of each story I'll ask if you think he made a good choice, and you can yell out "yes" or "no." Ready?

In the first story we see Peter when the soldiers have come to arrest Jesus and take him away to be crucified. Peter is with Jesus. Peter takes his sword and cuts off the ear of one of the men who have come for Jesus. Was this a good choice?

C: No!

L: After Jesus was arrested, Peter followed the soldiers to the place where Jesus was taken. When he went inside to be near Jesus, a girl standing in the doorway asked Peter, "Are you one of Jesus' disciples?" Peter lied and said, "No." Was this a good choice?

C: No!

L: While the religious leaders were questioning Jesus, Peter was waiting outside. Again someone asked him, "Are you one of Jesus' followers?" Again Peter lied and said, "No." Was that a good choice?

C: No!

L: As you can see, Peter didn't always tell the truth. He wasn't always peaceful. He didn't always make good choices. What about you? Are you always peaceful or truthful? Do you always make good choices?

C: *(Children may want to talk about times when they made bad choices, but be ready for them to be silent. Confessing faults is just as difficult for children as it is for adults!)*

L: No one except Jesus ever lived a perfect life. Everyone has done something to make Jesus sad, just like Peter. But Jesus forgave Peter, and after Jesus came back to life, he talked to Peter and gave him special instructions. *(Read John 21:15-17.)* When Jesus told Peter to "feed my sheep," Jesus was instructing Peter to tell others about him. Jesus loved Peter and knew he was sorry. Jesus knew Peter would do great work with God's power. Do you think we're all a little bit like Peter?

C: Yes.

L: Me too, I know I am! We all make mistakes. But Jesus loves us, too. We can tell Jesus we are sorry. We can turn away from doing the things that make Him sad and turn back to do great work with his power—just like Peter. Let's pray together and thank God for forgiving us . . . *(prayer).*

Heather Hagler

Four Stations of the Font

Scripture: Psalm 42:1-2; John 7:37-38; Psalm 1:1, 3; Hebrews 10:19, 22; Matthew 3:11

Season/Sunday: Any, but probably a baptism Sunday

Focus: The sermon focuses on four of the five meanings of baptism. The fifth (dying to self and rising with Christ) could be added depending on the context and theological views of the congregation, but might be a difficult concept to deal with otherwise.

Experience: The children will enact each of four scriptures dealing with the meaning of baptism, as read by the congregation. This sermon was also originally done as a baptism journey, working our way from the church entry toward the baptismal font.

Arrangements: You will need: (1) a tray with cups of water at the back of the room, in sufficient number for each child to have one, (2) a shower head (unscrewing one from home shouldn't be too difficult), and (3) water in the baptismal font. You will also need to arrange for the scripture verses to be printed in the bulletin in order to facilitate congregational participation. The announcement might read as follows:

> *Please participate in the children's sermon by reading each of these verses aloud in unison when prompted to do so. Thanks!*

As a deer longs for flowing streams,
  so my soul longs for you, O God.
My soul thirsts for God, for the living God. (Psalm 42:1-2)
Let anyone who is thirsty come to me, and let the one who believes in me drink. (John 7:37-38)

Happy are those
  who do not follow the advice of the wicked,

or take the path that sinners tread . . .
They are like trees
 planted by streams of water,
which yield their fruit in its season,
 and their leaves do not wither. (Psalm 1:1, 3)

Since we have confidence to enter the sanctuary by the blood of
Jesus . . . let us approach with a true heart in full assurance of
faith, with our hearts sprinkled clean from an evil conscience and
our bodies washed with pure water. (Hebrews 10:19, 22)

I baptize you with water for repentance, but one who is more powerful than I is coming after me . . . He will baptize you with the
Holy Spirit and fire. (Matthew 3:11)

Leader: *(From the back of the room.)* Good morning! I'd like
all of the children to join me back at the main
doors—we're going on a journey! Great to see you all
today, and I've got a question for you: if you were out
walking in the desert, and you went a long, long way,
would you be thirsty?

Children: Yes!

L: That's right! And that's sometime how we feel when
we come into church—we've been out walking
around in the desert of the world, and we come in
here, and it's wonderful because we know we're about
to be refreshed. And in fact, that's one of the meanings of baptism, the way we long for God and get refreshed in God's presence. We're going to ask the
congregation to read a couple of Bible verses that talk
about that, and while they do, we're going to drink
some refreshing water *(prompt congregation to do the
first reading while you serve the children from the
tray of water)*. Was that refreshing?

C: Yes!

L: Okay, let's move on in our baptismal journey *(no
need to go too far—head ten feet or so down the
main aisle)*. Okay, now we're going to pretend to be
trees, and if we're trees we have roots that go down in
search of what?

C: Dirt. Food. Water.

L: Water is what I was looking for, so while the congregation reads another verse, let's pretend we are trees, str-e-e-tching down our roots, and reeeeaching up to the heavens with our branches *(prompt second congregational reading while enacting)*.

   Good! Let's keep moving on our journey *(move another ten feet)* and now, I don't know about you, but all this dry dusty travel and roots in the ground and such, well, it all makes me feel like I need to get cleaned up, and that's another meaning of baptism. In baptism we are washing off the dirt of sin. And, I just happen to have a showerhead here, so while the congregation reads the next verse, let's get cleaned up! *(Prompt reading and take pretend shower.)* That was great—don't you feel better now?

C: Yes!

L: Okay, the last little bit of our journey *(move to baptismal font)* brings us to where we baptize people. We're not going to be baptized again, but let's all be reminded of our baptism by putting our hands on our heads while the congregation reads the last verse *(prompt reading and hand motion; if you're feeling particularly bold you might playfully splash a small amount of water on the children as the reading ends!)*. Wow, did you know that baptism has all those meanings?

C: Yes. No.

L: Let's have a prayer and thank God for using this sacrament to speak to our hearts, minds, and bodies in so many ways . . . *(prayer)*.

Brant D. Baker

Growing Grapes

Scripture: John 15:5

Season/Sunday: Any

Focus: Jesus's sermon about the vine and the branches is a powerful word-picture of staying connected to him. In this sermon, children will learn how they can grow in Jesus.

Experience: Children will pantomime a story of grapes growing on a vine.

Arrangements: You'll need a Bible marked at the verse for the lesson.

Leader: Today I need your help to bring a story to life. You will be the pictures. You copy the actions I show you as I tell the story.
Once there was a beautiful garden that grew grapes. This kind of a garden is called a vineyard. In the vineyard there grew a large grapevine. (*Hold your arms out from your sides slightly bent. Tilt your hands and fingers upward so your arms and hands resemble a vine.*)

Children: (*Copy your motions throughout.*)

L: On that grapevine there were many branches. The grapevine was strong and could hold many branches. The food from the soil went up through the roots (*gently shake one leg then the other to show roots*) to the branches on the vine. As the sun shone on the vine (*place your arms over your head, touching your finger tips to form a circle*) and the rain watered the vine (*place your arms straight up over your head, then lower your arms slowly as you gently wiggle your fingers to mimic rain falling*), the vine sent the nourishment to the branches.

40

The vine and the branches grew. *(Place your arms again in the shape of a vine and stretch them a little higher to show growth.)*
Over time, fat grapes grew on the branches. *(Place your arms at your sides and stand them out from your body to show roundness.)*
One branch was not as big as the others. Its grapes were small. This branch was sad. *(Make your hands into fists. Place your fists close to your eyes and turn your hands at the wrists to show crying.)*
The little branch said, "I am so small. I'll never be big. I'll never grow fat, juicy grapes."
The strong vine spoke gently to the small branch and said, "You are smaller than the others now, but if you stay connected to me I'll give you food and water. You will grow and make juicy grapes. If you break away from me you'll lose your nourishment. You'll wither up and turn brown. Then you'll never grow grapes. Just stay with me, and you'll be strong and healthy."
The person who told this story of the vine and branches was Jesus. When he told this story, he wasn't giving gardening lessons. He was teaching about himself and his followers. What do you think this story means?

C: *(Children share their thoughts.)*

L: *(Read John 15:5.)* In this story Jesus is telling us that if we want to do special work for God we have to stay close to him. How can we stay close to Jesus?

C: Pray. Read the Bible. Come to church?

L: Have you ever sat in church and thought, "I'm just a kid; I'll never do anything special for God"? Have you ever felt like the small branch in the story?

C: *(Allow children to share their feelings.)*

L: Jesus said if we stay close to him we will bear fruit, no matter how old we are. Does that mean if we pray and read our Bibles we'll grow grapes out of our fingers?

C: No!

L: No. When Jesus said we would bear fruit, he meant our lives and our actions would please God. When we bear fruit for God we do good things for God in this world. Let's have a prayer and ask Jesus to help us stay connected to him so we can grow strong and work for God's kingdom . . . *(prayer).*

Heather Hagler

Wow for Moms!

Scripture: Exodus 20:12

Season/Sunday: Mother's Day

Focus: Mother's Day is an especially good day for honoring mothers and celebrating the ways they influence our lives.

Experience: The leader will print the letters "M" "O" "M" on a sign and then ask the children what word the letters spell. Then the leader will flip the sign upside-down, telling the children that the letters now form a word that describes moms—"WOW." Finally, kids will participate in a Wow Litany in honor of their moms. (In the prayer or at another point during the sermon, you may want to acknowledge other women—grandmothers, foster-mothers, or other caregivers—who serve in the role of mother).

Arrangements: You will need a large piece of poster board or paper, and a marker or crayon that makes a bold line visible from a distance. Practice writing "MOM" in capital letters so that, when turned upside down, the letters form the word "WOW."

Leader:	Hello! I've got poster board and markers today because I'm going to write three important letters for you. *(Slowly write the letters that spell "MOM," pausing after each letter and asking the children to say the name of that letter.)* These letters spell an important word. And what is that word?
Children:	Mom!
L:	Yes. Mom! And why do you suppose we are thinking about moms, today of all days?
C:	Today is Mother's Day.
L:	Yes, today is Mother's Day. One of the Ten Commandments is, "Honor your father and your mother."

Even though it's important to honor your mother every day, Mother's Day is a special day set aside to honor mothers. I'm going to flip my sign upside-down to make a brand new word that describes moms *(flip the sign)*. What does my sign say now?

C: Wow!

L: Yes, "Wow"! And *wow* is a good word to describe our moms and the many ways they show us their love and their care. In honor of moms and Mother's Day, this morning we're going to say a Wow Litany. I'll say a line and then hold up my sign. Then all of you will shout "wow" in your happiest, most enthusiastic, Mother's Day voices. *(Practice holding up the sign a few times and leading the children in shouting "wow." Begin the litany.)*

L: Moms pray for us.

C: Wow!

L: Moms take care of us when we are sick.

C: Wow!

L: Moms cook good food for us.

C: Wow!

L: Moms play games and sing songs with us.

C: Wow!

L: Moms laugh and cry with us.

C: Wow!

L: Moms tuck us into bed at night.

C: Wow!

L: Moms wake us up in the morning with happy voices.

C: Wow!

L: Moms help us with our homework.

C: Wow!

L: Moms celebrate holidays with us.

C: Wow!

L: Moms hug us tight.

C: Wow!

L: And congregation, please join in this final "wow." Moms love us every single day.

All: Wow!

L: *(Turn the sign back around to read "MOM.")* So today, give your mom a really big hug and say,

"Wow! I love you Mom." Let's say a prayer thanking God for mothers and for all women who do a lot of these amazing things even when they aren't mothers . . . *(prayer).*

Barbara Younger

When Things Get Bumpy

Scripture: Mark 4:35-41

Season/Sunday: Any

Focus: Because Jesus has power over all things we never need to be afraid.

Experience: The children will pretend they are on a rocky boat and reenact the lesson.

Arrangements: Consider cutting a boat out of cardboard and have the kids get behind it. This might add to the experience for them. You could also bring in a pair of oars and a big net. Prior to the sermon ask one of the older children to pretend to be Jesus sleeping during the storm. Cue him or her when to say, "Peace! Be still!" You may also want to coach one of the children, who will be one of the disciples on the boat, to act as a leader for the other children when the story is reenacted. The congregation can be involved in this sermon by adding sound effects for the weather.

Leader: Good morning girls and boys!
Children: Good morning!
L: Our gospel lesson for this morning tells us that Jesus was in a boat with his disciples going across a lake. There were other boats going with them. All the boats were caught in a really big storm. It was so stormy that the boat was tossed around and water started to get in it. What do you think people would be doing if they were on a really rocky boat that was starting to fill up with water?
C: They would be scared. They might be screaming. Bouncing all over. Hanging onto the boat to stay in it.
L: Let's practice what it might look like to be on a boat in a rough storm.

C: *(Pretending to be tossed around.)* WHOA! Hold on! This is scary!

L: That's right! Now let's pretend we are on the boat with Jesus, too. Jump onto the boat. "Sarah" is going to pretend to be Jesus asleep on the boat during the storm. The rest of you can be the scared disciples on the rocky boat. Think about what you would do if Jesus were on the boat with you. Here comes the storm! *(Make wind and storm sounds, congregation could be invited to assist.)*

C: I'm scared! I can't stand up! WHOA! Wake up, Jesus! Wake up!

Sarah: What's happening?

C: We're in a bad storm! Save us! Save us!

Sarah: I say to the storm: "Peace, be still!"

C: Yay! Jesus saved us!

L: That sure looked like it was a pretty bumpy ride!

C: It sure was!

L: Sometimes we have rough and bumpy times in life, too, when things are scary and don't go well. Can you name some times that you've been scared?

C: In a thunderstorm. When my cat ran away. When I got lost in a store. In the dark.

L: Those are some pretty scary things, aren't they? Well, today we hear in the lesson that we don't need to be afraid even when things get bumpy because Jesus will always be with us, just like he was with the disciples. And when we get scared, he can calm us, too. Let's say a prayer to help us remember that Jesus has power over all things and we never need to be afraid . . . *(prayer)*.

Susan M. Lang

Transfiguration

Scripture: Mark 9:2-9

Season/Sunday: Transfiguration

Focus: What might Jesus say to me?

Experience: Using an ancient practice associated with Ignatius of Loyola (AD 1491–1556), the children will be invited to use their spiritual imagination to picture what happened on the mountain during the transfiguration and to listen for Jesus to speak to them.

Arrangements: Practice leading a guided meditation, adjusting the rhythm to your natural way of speaking. This would be an easy sermon to invite the congregation to participate in as well.

Leader:	Today we are going to use our spiritual imaginations. Sometimes it is easier to use our imaginations with our eyes closed, so let's close our eyes. Now let's use our imaginations to picture a mountain. You are picturing a mountain in your imagination and you have to decide if it is big or small, and whether it's covered with rocks or grass or trees *(pause)*. Now open your eyes, and raise your hand if you had a really big mountain?
Children:	*(Children raise hands in response to questions throughout.)*
L:	Yeah, lots of those. How many had a grassy mountain? Oh, just a few of those. Who had lots of rocks? Not many there. How many of you had snow on your mountain? Look at all the people with snow.
	Okay, now let's close our eyes again and get our imaginations ready, and this time imagine you see Jesus on your mountain. And as you see Jesus, pay

attention to what he looks like—whether he is tall or short, whether he has blonde hair or dark hair, whether he is happy or sad *(pause)*. Okay, now open your eyes and let's see what we imagined. How many of you saw Jesus as tall?

C: *(Children raise hands as before.)*

L: How many saw him with blonde hair? How many saw dark hair? Oh, a lot of those! How many of you saw Jesus with a beard? Not too many of those. Did any of you have a fat Jesus? That's okay too. You are good at this so let's try again.

Close your eyes and imagine your mountain and Jesus is up on that mountain. And with Jesus are a few of his friends: Peter, James, and John are up there with him, and they are all standing around on the mountain *(pause)*. All of a sudden Moses and Elijah show up, so now there are five friends up there with Jesus, and if you want, you can put yourself into the picture too *(pause)*. Now, Jesus' clothes start to sparkle or glow or shine. Can you see that in your imagination? Then all of a sudden you hear a voice say, "This is my Son, the Beloved; listen to him!" You and the other five people up there don't know what to think about that *(pause)*. Now imagine that Jesus walks over to you. There you are and there is Jesus. Jesus is right there with you and he leans over and whispers in your ear. *(Make a whispering sound.)* He's telling you something special just for you. Listen to what Jesus whispers to you *(pause)*.

Let's have a prayer and give thanks for being given hearts to love, minds to think, and imaginations to see and know and hear Jesus . . . *(prayer)*.

Karen Evans

Promises

Scripture: Acts 2:14-18; John 14:15-17

Season/Sunday: Pentecost

Focus: Making and keeping promises are very important to children. When the children learn that Jesus always keeps his promises, their trust in him will grow.

Experience: The leader will read a list of people in the children's lives, including Jesus. The children will give a thumbs-up if that person always keeps promises, a thumbs-sideways if that person sometimes keeps promises, and a thumbs-down if that person never keeps promises.

Arrangements: No special preparation is needed for this sermon.

Leader: Today we're going to talk together about promises. Raise your hand if you make promises.
Children: *(Most will raise their hands.)*
L: What kinds of promises do you make?
C: I promised to keep a secret. I promised my mom I would clean my room. I promised my grandmother I would eat all my vegetables.
L: Do you keep your promises?
C: Yes. Sometimes.
L: Do other people make promises to you? Do they keep their promises?
C: *(Give the children a chance to share their answers.)*
L: Let's play a game to think about making and keeping promises. I'll name some people who make promises. If this person always keeps promises, you give me a thumbs-up sign *(demonstrate)*. If the person I name sometimes keeps promises, show me a thumbs-

sideways sign *(demonstrate)*. If this person never keeps promises, give me a thumbs-down sign *(demonstrate)*. Ready, here we go:
• The wolf in "Little Red Riding Hood"
• Spider-Man
• Jafar in *Aladdin*
• Your friends
• *(List other popular superheroes and villains, and perhaps some of the individuals they named when talking about other people. Try to avoid putting the children in a bind. This could happen if you listed parents or teachers, who ought to keep promises, but don't always. Avoid naming these important role models who may fail from time to time. Finish with the name of Jesus.)*
• Jesus

    Today we celebrate Pentecost. Does anyone know why we are celebrating Pentecost?

C: *(Some of the children may know about the birthday of the church.)*

L: Pentecost is the day Jesus kept one of his promises. Jesus promised the disciples that after he went up into heaven, he would send God's Spirit, called the Holy Spirit, to be with the disciples and help them. On Pentecost, Jesus kept his promise and the Holy Spirit came to the disciples. Jesus makes that same promise of the Holy Spirit to us. He promised God's Spirit would help everyone who wants to follow God's commands. Jesus keeps his promise even today. Can you think of other promises Jesus has made?

C: *(Responses might include: to be with us always, to help us when we are afraid, to show us how to obey God, or to take us to heaven when we die.)*

L: Does Jesus keep his promises?

C: Yes!

L: Jesus keeps every promise he has ever made—not just some of them, but all of them. Let's have a prayer and give thanks that we can trust what Jesus says because he always keeps his promises . . . *(prayer).*

Heather Hagler

Good News or Bad News

Scripture: Romans 8:28

Season/Sunday: Any

Focus: Both bad and good things happen in life but "all things work together for good for those who love God."

Experience: Children will help tell a story of good news and bad news.

Arrangements: Prepare a good news/bad news story. You may want to use the classic good news/bad news story from China entitled "The man who lost his horse" as presented below (taken from http://chinapage.com/story/losthorse.html), or use Margery Cuyler's book, *That's Good! That's Bad!* (New York: Henry Holt, 1993), or even use a story you make up yourself.

> **Leader:** Today I'd like to tell you a story and I need your help. Whenever I move to this side and pause I need all of you to say, "That's good," and when I move over to this side and pause I need all of you to say, "That's bad." Let's practice one time *(walk to one side)*.
>
> **Children:** That's good!
>
> **L:** *(Walk to the other side.)*
>
> **C:** That's bad!
>
> **L:** That was great, so let's get started! Once upon a time a man living in China lost his treasured horse *(walk to "bad" side and pause)*.
>
> **C:** That's bad.
>
> **L:** No, that's good. You see a few months later the horse showed up leading another fine horse *(walk to opposite side and pause)*.
>
> **C:** That's good!

L: No really, that's bad. You see the man's son who liked to ride, was riding the new horse one day and fell off and broke his leg *(walk to other side and pause)*.

C: That's bad.

L: Well, no really, that's good. You see a few months later they came to the town to force all the young men to go and fight in the army, but because the son had a broken leg he could not go and was saved from death *(walk to other side and pause)*.

C: That's good.

L: Yes, that was good, and there is a verse in the Bible that talks about things working out this way. I'll say a few words and then you repeat after me, "We know that all things *(pause for echo)*, work together for good *(pause)*, for those who love God . . . " *(pause)*.

You know sometimes good things happen and sometimes bad things happen to all of us, but the good news is that God works in everything that happens to ultimately make it come out good. It may not look good to us at the moment, and that's because it probably isn't good, but God in Christ is faithful and uses even bad things to accomplish a good purpose in the lives of those who love God. Let's have a prayer giving thanks that we worship such a powerful God, that even the bad things that happen can be used for good . . . *(prayer)*.

Karen Evans

Name That Hymn!

Scripture: Colossians 3:16b

Season/Sunday: Any

Focus: We worship God by singing hymns.

Experience: Children will be introduced to a guest musician before enjoying a game called Name That Hymn. After listening to the first few notes of each hymn, they will try to guess which hymn the musician is playing.

Arrangements: Invite a musician in your congregation to help with this sermon. The instrument can be the piano or organ, or a hand-held instrument such as a flute or violin. Invite the children to sit close and watch the musician play. Choose—or ask your guest musician to choose—hymns the children in your church know. (You may want to include one or two Christmas carols since children can often recognize them at a young age.) Depending on how much time is allotted for the sermon, you will need about four to eight hymns. Explain to your guest musician that he or she is to play the first few notes of the hymn and then pause. If the children can't guess the hymn after hearing those notes, you will ask the musician to play a few more. As the worship service is planned, consider having the congregation sing one or more of the hymns used in Name That Hymn.

Leader: Good morning! I'm so excited because today "Mark" is our special guest, and he is going to help us play Name That Hymn! He'll play a few notes of a hymn on his "accordion", and you raise your hand as soon as you think you know the hymn.

Musician: *(Plays hymns as indicated. You may want to ask the musician to play the entire hymn or at least the first line or two, once the children have guessed it.)*

Children: *(Guess hymns.)*
    L: It's fun to recognize some of our favorite hymns. Can you name other favorite hymns?
    C: *(Various responses.)*
    L: Let's ask the congregation for their ideas too!
Congregation: *(Various responses.)*
    L: Why do we sing hymns?
    C: Because they are part of church. Because they are fun. To worship God.
    L: One of the ways we worship God is by singing hymns. Paul wrote in a letter to the Colossian church, "With gratitude in your hearts sing psalms, hymns, and spiritual songs to God." Since the early days of the church, Christians have sung hymns when they have gathered for worship. When you grow up, you will remember the hymns you sang in this church and they will be very special to you. Let's say a prayer thanking God for hymns, especially the hymns we love to sing together . . . *(prayer)*.

Barbara Younger

Blessing

Scripture: Numbers 6:24-26

Season/Sunday: Father's Day; could also be used for Mother's Day

Focus: The sermon looks at the biblical practice of blessing one another.

Experience: Both children and parents will learn and experience the three parts of the meaning of blessing. The information on blessing comes from *The Blessing* by Gary Smalley and John Trent (Nashville: Thomas Nelson, 1993).

Arrangements: None are needed other than to have a copy of the Aaronic blessing in hand when doing the sermon.

> **Leader:** Good morning! I'd like to invite the children to come forward and bring with them their father, grandfather, or another significant male; or if they're not here, with whomever they came with this morning. *(After group assembles.)* This morning we're going to learn about the biblical practice of blessing. Can anyone think of a time when they have been blessed?
>
> **Children:** When I was baptized? When I sneeze? When we say grace?
>
> **L:** Maybe so! Well, in the olden days of the Bible people often blessed one another, and especially their children. Would you like to receive a blessing today?
>
> **C:** Yes!
>
> **L:** All right, well the first part of a blessing is being touched in a meaningful way. Parents, this usually meant placing the right hand on the head or shoulder of the one being blessed because the right hand was the hand of blessing and strength. *(Encourage the*

adults present to place their right hand on the head of their child.) Good! Okay, the second part of blessing is to speak a meaningful word, to say something that suggests a special future for the person being blessed. Now, I'm going to lead us in a blessing in just a moment, but later on today you may want to add to what we say here. Also, another way to think about "speaking a meaningful word as blessing," might be praise, which family experts tell us is more important than criticism in shaping young lives. Okay, parents, we're going to use the blessing of Aaron this morning and so if you would, please repeat after me:
The LORD bless you and keep you; *(pause for echo)*
the LORD make his face *(echo)*
to shine upon you, and be gracious to you; *(echo)*
the LORD lift up his countenance upon you, *(echo)*
and give you peace *(echo)*.

L: Finally, blessings include an active commitment to see that these words come to pass by the one bestowing the blessing, and that's the ongoing job of being a parent! Let's have a prayer and thank God we can bless one another so much . . . *(prayer)*.

Brant D. Baker

Name-sake?

Scripture: 3 John 7 (NIV); Philippians 2:9-10 (NIV)

Season/Sunday: Any

Focus: This sermon focuses on the name of Jesus and the importance of the name.

Experience: Children will help solve the mystery of 3 John 7 by searching for a clue.

Arrangements: If your worship area has a large pulpit Bible, then you should plan to use it to solve the mystery of the name. If not, plan to carry a Bible yourself as you go out in search of the clue. Arrange ahead of time for someone to bring a study Bible with a concordance to worship. On cue, this volunteer will look up the word *name* in the concordance, and find the reference to Philippians 2:9-10, thus providing the clue. A cape and magnifying glass would be fun props for the leader!

> **Leader:** Hello kids, I'm so glad to see you today! Today there is a mystery afoot, and I am going to need your help. 3 John, verse 7 says, "It was for the sake of the Name that they went out . . . " Will you help me find a clue to solve the mystery of the name?
>
> **Children:** Yes! Okay!
>
> **L:** Good. Let's think about this *(repeating verse slowly)*, "It was for the sake of the Name that they went out." Aha! So they "went out." I guess that means we should go out too *(get up and start walking into the worship area)*. And they went out "for the sake of the Name." And that's the mystery, isn't it? We've got to find a clue to know what the name is. Well what are you waiting for *(hands on hips)*? We've got a mystery

to solve. Come on, we're going out to look for a clue *(motion for the kids to join you)*! *(Note: if one of the children suggests that the name might be "Jesus," cover by saying, "That could be, but we aren't sure yet!")* Maybe we can find a clue under here *(lean down to look under an unoccupied pew or chair)*. Do you think we can find out what the name is, under here?

C: *(Engage in the search.)*

L: Hmmm. I wonder if it is up in one of these windows?

C: No!

L: Well, could it be behind your ear?

C: *(Laughter.)* No!

L: Well then, we only have one more place to look. *(Turn to the congregation.)* Does anyone have a study Bible with a concordance?

Volunteer: I do!

L: That's great because a concordance is a list that tells us where different words are used in the Bible. *(To the volunteer.)* Will you look up the word *name* and give us a clue as to where we can look. *(Begin rubbing your hands together in delight.)* I think this is going to work, don't you?

C: Yes!

Volunteer: The word *name* shows up in Philippians 2:9-10.

L: I knew it! The Bible gives clues to help us understand the Bible! Let's look it up! *(Hurry to the pulpit Bible, or use another one.)* Here it is, repeat these words after me: "Therefore God exalted him to the highest place *(pause for echo)* and gave him the name that is above every name *(pause)*, that at the name of Jesus *(pause)* every knee should bow" (Philippians 2:9-10).

So! The mystery of the name is solved! *(Reverently.)* I think we need to kneel like the verse says, and let's have a prayer thanking God for the name of Jesus . . . *(prayer)*.

Bob Sharman

Reasons to Celebrate!

Scripture: Psalm 117 (CEV)

Season/Sunday: Sunday before the Fourth of July

Focus: The children will discover four reasons to honor and celebrate our nation's birthday, including the freedom of worship.

Experience: This sermon involves the children in Q&A, singing a holiday song to the tune of "If You're Happy and You Know It," and reviewing the reasons to celebrate with quick and easy hand motions.

Arrangements: None are needed, unless you feel uncomfortable with singing. In that case, ask a choir member to assist you. Photocopy the sermon for that person to follow. You will lead the children's response to encourage them. You can also ask the congregation to assist with the singing as a way to involve them as well.

  Leader: Hi! It's great to see you! Do you know what holiday we're celebrating soon (today)?

 Children: The Fourth of July!

    L: Yes! On the Fourth of July in 1776, our nation declared independence from England. The people of the thirteen colonies wanted to be free. Because England did not want them to break away, the two sides fought many battles, even at night. Sometimes the dark sky was full of flaring rockets and bursting cannonballs. What bright, exploding lights do we see on the night of our Fourth of July celebrations?

    C: Fireworks!

    L: Yes! These fireworks are supposed to remind us of the battles fought for our freedom. Let's honor our freedom with a little song. I'll sing the first line, and then you repeat it, then I'll sing the rest. Ready?

C: Ready.

L: *(Sung to the tune of "If You're Happy And You Know It.")*
On the Fourth of July, watch the fireworks!

C: On the Fourth of July, watch the fireworks!

L: On the Fourth of July, look at the starburst sky;
On the Fourth of July, watch the fireworks!

C: *(Could repeat last line: "On the Fourth of July, watch the fireworks!" If you use this option, arrange a hand signal cue to indicate which lines the children should echo.)*

L: Very good! Here's a new question for you—does our nation have a flag?

C: Yes!

L: What does it look like?

C: It has stars and stripes. It's red, white, and blue. It has fifty stars.

L: You're right! In 1818, our Congress passed the Flag Act to make sure that all the flags in the United States looked exactly the same. Before that time, a number of different American flags were flown. The Flag Act said that every flag should have thirteen stripes and a star for each state. It also said that if a new state was added to our nation, the new star could not be put on the flag until the Fourth of July. Can you tell me ways that we honor our flag on the Fourth?

C: Fly it. Wave it. Decorate with it.

L: Yes! Let's show how much we appreciate our flag with another verse of our song. Ready?
On the Fourth of July, wave a flag!

C: On the Fourth of July, wave a flag!

L: On the Fourth of July, you can see our colors fly!
On the Fourth of July, wave a flag!

C: *(Optional echo.)* On the Fourth of July, wave a flag!

L: Are there other ways you like to celebrate the Fourth?

C: Going to a parade. Going to the fair. Decorating. Having a picnic.

L: Those all sound like fun! In the United States, we have the wonderful freedom to get together with other people to do these things. It's called the right of assembly. And we have another important freedom, the freedom to worship God. It's great to know we're free to come here and worship together. I think we have another reason to sing:
On the Fourth of July, worship God!

C: On the Fourth of July, worship God!

L: On the Fourth of July, pray to our God Most High!
On the Fourth of July, worship God!

C: *(Optional echo.)* On the Fourth of July, worship God!

L: Okay, let's remember the ways to celebrate on the Fourth. I'll say it and show it, and then you'll do it. We watch fireworks *(tilt head up, shade eyes with hand; invite children to do the same)*; we wave flags *(close fist, wave back and forth)*; we have fun *(wave hands above head)*; and we worship God *(fold hands in prayer)*.

Nice! Now it's time to bow our heads. I'll read Psalm 117 for our prayer: "All of you nations, come praise the Lord! Let everyone praise him. His love for us is wonderful; his faithfulness never ends. Shout praises to the Lord!" And let the people say: Amen!

All: Amen!

Lisa Flinn

Getting Our Attention

Scripture: Exodus 3:1-12

Season/Sunday: Any

Focus: By using a burning bush, God got Moses' attention and called him to a special job to lead God's people out of Egypt into a new land. God calls you and me to do special things, too. How does God get our attention when asking us to serve?

Experience: The children will talk about how God gets their attention to serve God, and about special jobs that God might be calling them to do.

Arrangements: Invite each child to come forward with a parent or trusted adult. Give these adults a picture of a burning bush and then ask them to move to somewhere in the sanctuary (for example, along the outer aisles or into the narthex).

Leader: Today we heard about Moses. God had a special job for Moses and wanted Moses to lead God's people out of Egypt where they were slaves and were forced to build cities for the Egyptians. But Moses was far away from Egypt. So one day God got Moses' attention with a bush that was burning. Usually when something catches on fire, it totally burns up and will even turn to ash. This one didn't! It was so strange that it got Moses' attention. Have you ever seen anything really strange that got your attention?

Children: Yes! *(You can expect anything here!)*

L: While I suppose that God could still use something really strange to get our attention today, that doesn't usually happen. Instead of using burning bushes, God often works through the people around us to invite us

to do special jobs. Have any of you ever been asked
to help out with a special job?

C: I once sat with my Grandmother when she wasn't
feeling well. I take out the trash.

L: Those are really special jobs! So my question for you
is how does God get our attention today and ask us
to do special jobs?

C: I don't know.

L: Sometimes your parents may ask for help with things.
Or maybe there is a special food drive at church or a
collection of items for people in need. Maybe you
might see your brother or sister crying and they might
need help. God gets our attention through other people. So it's important that we pay attention to people
around us and see how we might help them.

Well, let's do this: let's all pretend to be Moses. We
are out wandering in the wilderness, and we come
across a burning bush. Now, go find the person who
came up here with you, and take just a minute or two
to think together about some of the special things that
you do to serve God. Then write them down on the
burning bush picture. You can take it home and hang
it up so that you'll remember how you serve God,
too. *(Give children a chance to disperse and interact
with parent.)*

(After a minute or two.) I hope you will keep talking about this later today, but right now let's say a
prayer to thank God that we each have a special job
to do . . . *(prayer).*

Susan M. Lang

Friend Puzzle

Scripture: Proverbs 17:17

Season/Sunday: Any

Focus: Friends play an influential role in our lives. When we know the qualities of a good friend, we can choose our friends wisely and be a better friend.

Experience: As a group the children will create a living-friend puzzle by using bodies. This puzzle will help them discuss the qualities of a good friend.

Arrangements: Instruct the children to clear a wide place on the floor in the Children's Sermon area where everyone can see. If you have a small group of children, ask some adults to join your group and complete the puzzle. As presented here, you will need 13 "body parts." As you read each part of the puzzle and its description, call up a child or children to lie on the floor to create the puzzle. Be sure to think about how many children you normally have for a children's sermon and have enough body parts ready in case a few extra show up! You may want to arrange to have someone photograph this "floor art" for later display!

Leader: Good morning! Let me read you a verse from Proverbs, a Bible book of wisdom. The verse says, "A friend loves at all times." Raise your hand and each of you can take turns telling me the name of one of your friends.

Children: *(Tell the names of their friends.)*

L: We're going to put together a puzzle that will help us think about what makes a good friend. You are all going to be the pieces. We'll put the friend puzzle together on the floor. First, we need a brain. The brain of a good friend will help you think of solutions to problems and will help you think of ways to have fun. Who will be the brain in this friend?

C: I will! *(Have a child curl up in a ball on the floor to be the brain.)*

L: On either side of the brain we have ears. Who will be our ears?

C: Me! I will! *(On either side of the "brain," have two children lie in semicircles to look like ears.)*

L: A good friend's ears will listen to a joke or to your worries. On the head we also have eyes. Who will be our eyes?

C: We will! *(Under the "brain," have two children curl up in balls to be the eyes.)*

L: The eyes of a good friend will help to see if trouble is coming. They'll also see your best, new shoes. Okay, next we have a mouth—any volunteers?

C: I'm a mouth. *(Have a child lie under the eyes, in a semicircle, to be a mouth.)*

L: A good friend's mouth will never tell your secrets. Another piece of a good friend is the heart. Who can be the heart?

C: Me! *(Have a child lie under the mouth, curled up in a ball, to be the heart.)*

L: The heart of a good friend will trust you. Now we need arms and legs—any limbs left?

C: I guess we can. *(Have two children lay straight on the floor diagonally from the heart for the arms, the other two running down from the heart to be the legs.)*

L: A good friend's arms can help pull you along when you're climbing up a steep hill, and their legs will stand up for you if someone picks on you. The last part of a good friend we'll talk about today are the feet. We need a couple of feet, about size 47.

C: Us! *(Have two children curl in a ball under each leg to be feet.)*

L: The feet of a good friend will be ready to run and play with you. Wow—you look like a good friend! And now we know what it takes for us to be a good friend too! Let's all sit up and have a prayer giving thanks that God has given us good friends in our lives . . . *(prayer).*

Heather Hagler

Sundays Are for Worship

Scripture: Genesis 2:2-3

Season/Sunday: Any Sunday

Focus: Sundays are a special day to worship God.

Experience: Children will visually see the connection between those who lead worship and those who participate in worship, and they will experience leading the congregation in a song.

Arrangements: Prompt the choir and other persons who lead worship to be prepared to stand when they are asked. Decide on a song for the children to lead.

Leader: Good morning! I'm glad that you are all here on this Sunday. I have two special verses I'd like to read to you. *(Read Genesis 2:2-3.)* What day of the week does the scripture say that God rested?

Children: The seventh day. Saturday.

L: The people of Jesus' day worshiped together on Saturday, and today some people gather to worship on Saturday. Why do you suppose we worship together on Sunday?

C: *(Various responses.)*

L: The first Christians decided to meet together on the day of the week that Jesus rose from the dead. That day was like a mini-Easter to them. They also worshiped on Saturday with the Jewish community. Later they dropped the Saturday worship and met together on Sundays. What do you like best about our worship time?

C: *(Various responses.)*

L: We call the special things that we do in worship *liturgy.* That word comes from two Greek words that mean "people" and "work." And so what we do here on Sunday mornings might be called the work of the people. Why do you suppose we have a platform here at the front of our worship room?

C: *(Various responses.)*

L: One reason we have a raised platform is so that everyone can see those who are leading worship. It doesn't mean that the people on the platform are any more important than anyone else, because we are all special to God. Worship is something like a play, but in a different way than most plays. In most plays the actors are on the stage and the people are the audience and just watch. *(Ask the choir and others on the platform to stand up.)* In worship, however, all of the people on the platform are actually the prompters or coaches. They are important because they help us worship. And who do we worship?

C: God. Jesus.

L: That's right. God or Jesus is the audience. Who, then, are the actors?

C: The people.

L: Will the real actors of worship please stand up? *(Indicate that the congregation should stand.)* Now children, you and I are going to be the prompters and lead the people in an act of worship. We will lead them in singing *(name of song)*. *(Choose a song that the children are familiar with.)* That was great! Let's have a prayer thanking God that we can come together to worship . . . *(prayer).*

Delia Halverson

Walking in the Truth

Scripture: 3 John 4 (NIV)

Season/Sunday: Any

Focus: This sermon focuses on what it can mean to walk in the truth.

Experience: Children will walk around and discover, then practice a prayer walk.

Arrangements: None required.

> **Leader:** Good morning, young disciples. Our sermon today is a hard one because we have to figure out what this verse means. Will you help me?
>
> **Children:** Yes!
>
> **L:** Okay, echo the verse after me: "I have no greater joy *(pause)*, than to hear that my children *(pause)*, are walking in the truth" *(pause)*.
> So, this verse says that children—that's us—bring joy, by what? Does anyone remember?
>
> **C:** Walking in the truth.
>
> **L:** But, how do we walk in the truth? That's the part I can't figure out. What do you think?
>
> **C:** *(Silence.)* I don't know.
>
> **L:** Well, I know about walking, so let's start by doing that. Everyone stand up and let's walk around. (*Begin walking contemplatively around the sanctuary.*) Are we walking in the truth yet?
>
> **C:** No. I don't think so.
>
> **L:** I don't think so either. Let's try this: instead of just walking around, let's do a prayer walk and ask Jesus to help us walk in the truth. What do you think?

C: Okay. That won't work.

L: Well, let's try: As we make our way back to where we started you can repeat after me, "Dear Jesus *(pause)*, help me to bring you joy *(pause)*. Help me to walk in the truth *(pause)*, help me to love the truth *(pause)*, and help me to love you *(pause)*. In your name we pray, amen *(pause)*."

Bob Sharman

Take a Walk

Scripture: Ephesians 5:15-20

Season/Sunday: Any

Focus: Things to watch out for as we walk the Christian walk.

Experience: Children will take a walk around the sanctuary.

Arrangements: You may want to arrange for a person to bump into you ahead of time, but that's probably not necessary. You will also want to know ahead of time who you will speak about as having meant a lot to you on your walk.

> **Leader:** You know, I really like taking walks. I think we can learn some things about walking with Jesus every day from what it is like to just take a walk. So let's take a walk. Everybody stand up and follow me *(start a walk around the sanctuary)*. When we go on a walk what are some things we have to do so our walk will be good? Like, what might you wear?
>
> **Children:** Tennis shoes. Sneakers.
>
> **L:** That's right, you'll want your feet to be comfortable, so you would not wear flip-flops because they would make your feet hurt. So you want good tennis shoes or hiking shoes.
>
> **C:** You might need a raincoat. Sunscreen.
>
> **L:** Sure *(picking up on whatever the children offer)*, depending on the weather you may need a raincoat or gloves. It seems to me that when we walk with Jesus we need to make sure we take certain things also, like our Bible, and maybe some hymns and Jesus songs. Those are all important things to take with us. Another important thing to remember when we are

walking *(as you say this, walk backwards and stumble or bump into someone)*—oh, I'm sorry! I wasn't watching where I was going.

(To the children.) You see when we go walking we must pay attention to where we are going because if we don't we could hurt ourselves or somebody else. And the same is true in our Christian walk. If we don't pay attention to where we are going and how we are living we could get hurt. You see there are some bad things out there in the world and we don't want to get into that bad stuff. We only want to do good stuff, so we better watch where we are going and what we are doing. Let's keep walking.

Now there is one other really important thing about taking a walk. That is, deciding whom you are going to walk with. That makes all the difference in the world. Walking with other people who also love Jesus makes all the difference in the world. I want to tell you about someone who has walked with me for a number of years and how wonderful it has been to walk with her. This is Miss Phyllis, and she has taught in our preschool and worked with our children for twenty years. Miss Phyllis loves Jesus, and I am so thankful that I have had Miss Phyllis to walk with all these years.

Let's all find someone to walk with us back up to the front for our closing prayer. It doesn't have to be one of your parents. Pick someone nearby who looks like they know Jesus.

C: *(Find people to walk with them to the front of the sanctuary.)*

L: Let's have a prayer and thank God that we have a whole church full of people who can help us remember to take the right things on our walk with Jesus, and who can go with us and help us do the right things along the way . . . *(prayer).*

Karen Evans

Walking in the Way

Scripture: Joshua 1:7; John 14:6

Season/Sunday: Any

Focus: The best or shortest way isn't always the easiest way, but as long as we are in Christ and following His word, we'll get there.

Experience: The children will determine a route across the sanctuary, only to have some unexpected barriers arise.

Arrangements: This sermon is written for sanctuaries that have at least three aisles: a center aisle and two side aisles. If your sanctuary has a different layout, some adaptation may be needed. Arrange to have written instructions in the bulletin, and plan to call the congregation's attention to those instructions as the children gather. The instructions could read as follows:

> Attention people along the center aisle: when the children's sermon leader says, "Okay, let's go," it will be your cue to stand up and move into the aisle, creating an unexpected traffic jam in the children's path. Thank you for your help!

Leader: Good morning! I'd like to invite the children to meet me at the back of the church. *(As children gather.)* It's great to see you this morning, and I have a question for you: what is the shortest, easiest, way for us to get from back here to up there *(indicate front of the church)*?

Children: This way *(should indicate center aisle)*!

L: Yes, I think you're right. But to be sure, let's go over here and just look more closely. *(Talking as you move.)* It's our goal to enter into God's presence and worship, and the best way looks like it is the center aisle. Let's go over to the other side and check that

73

one too *(moving across back to opposite side, continue talking)*. This reminds me of a verse in the book of Joshua where God tells Joshua that he and the people are to be very careful to do everything commanded of them by God's word, and not to turn from it to either the right *(indicate the right aisle)* or to the left *(indicate left aisle)*, so that they could have success wherever they go (Joshua 1:7). *(Having returned to the center.)* So do we all agree that the center aisle is the best?

C: Yes!

L: Okay, let's go.

Congregation: *(Following cue, move into center aisle.)*

L: Whoa, wait a minute! That was unexpected! Don't knock anyone over, but it looks like the shortest way just turned into the hardest way! *(Continue making progress—it may be necessary to remind children that it isn't a race, so that no one gets hurt!)* Wow, this reminds me of another Bible verse where Jesus says, "I am the way, and the truth, and the life. No one comes to the Father, except through me" (John 14:6). *(Arriving at the front.)* Whew! That was tough, but we did it! Let's have a prayer and give thanks that when we follow God's commandments and believe in Jesus Christ, we get to where we need to go . . . *(prayer)*.

Brant D. Baker

You Are a Breath of God

Scripture: Genesis 2:7

Season/Sunday: Any, or a baptism Sunday

Focus: We are vessels of God's spirit, containers for God's life-giving breath.

Experience: To have fun while remembering how God first breathed life into human beings.

Arrangements: Bubbles, any kind will do. You can pick them up at any dollar store. Also you will need a clear ball or a large, clear marble. One way to get bubbles and a clear ball together is to purchase a magic trick called Miracle Bubbles, available at most magic shops or online. Even though the sermon can be done without using a ball, it loses some of its educational punch and memorable drama. If you do use a ball, practice the sleight of hand a few times to pull off the effect.

Leader:	Good morning. How many of you like to blow bubbles? (*Have bubbles out and ready, holding the ball in your hand.*)
Children:	I do! I do!
L:	Me too! I like bubbles. I brought some with me today *(begin blowing bubbles).*
C:	*(May try to catch bubbles, which is fine.)*
L:	Bubbles are really fun. They come in all shapes and sizes. No two bubbles are alike *(continue to blow bubbles throughout).* Did you ever think that bubbles catch your breath for a little while, which allow them to float through the air? Have you ever tried to catch a bubble?
C:	Yes. No. You can't catch them—they blow up.

L: I know. Catching bubbles is hard to do. What if we could catch a bubble and hold onto it? Wouldn't that be neat?

C: Yeah, that would be cool!

L: Let's try that. I'm going to try to catch a bubble and hold onto it. *(Blow some more bubbles. Then, using the hand that is holding the clear ball, reach up and pretend to catch a bubble. Hold the ball up and show it to the kids and congregation. It looks like you caught a bubble and are now holding onto it.)* There, I caught one!

C: Wow, let me see! Do that again!

L: I think God likes bubbles. What if you could catch one of God's bubbles? What if there was a way to hold onto a little of the breath of God. Well, there is. The Bible says, "Then the LORD God formed [humans] from the dust of the ground, and breathed into [their] nostrils the breath of life; and the [human] became . . . living beings." That means *(putting ball away and picking up or pointing to one of the smaller children)* that *(Name)* is a breath of God. It means that *(Name)* is a breath God *(indicate another child)*. We are all containers for the life-giving breath of God. Let's pray and give thanks that God has put breath into us . . . *(prayer)*.

Jeff L. Hutcheson

Show and Tell

Scripture: Philippians 1:5 (NLT) and 1:27b (TLB)

Season/Sunday: Any

Focus: We are called to be people who both show God's love in Christ, and speak of it as well.

Experience: The children will be asked to perform a simple task, in this case filling the gap between people on opposite sides of the aisle, and then saying why they did so.

Arrangements: None are needed.

> **Leader:** Good morning! Let me read to you two Bible verses from the book of Philippians: "You've been my partners in spreading the Good News about Christ. " said the Apostle Paul (Philippians 1:5). "You are standing together side by side with one strong purpose—to tell the Good News" (Philippians 1:27b). I wonder if you would be willing to partner with me this morning to help these people out here *(motion to congregation)* get connected? Would you do that?
>
> **Children:** Yes!
>
> **L:** Fantastic! Well, let's ask "Emily" to be our first volunteer. Emily, the people on this side of the aisle really want to be connected with the people on that side of the aisle, but they can't quite reach *(indicate to the people sitting on the ends of opposite rows to reach out toward one another)*. But if you stood right here between them, and took their hands, they'd be connected.
>
> **Emily:** Like this *(joins hands)*?
>
> **L:** Exactly—that's perfect! Now that we've seen how it's done, can the rest of you help join the rest of these people who are on opposite sides of the aisle?

C: *(Move into their assignment—it would be nice and orderly if you started with the last row and moved forward, but it likely won't work that way!)*

L: Be sure to let the people through who still have to move to the back! *(After a few moments to get organized.)* Is everybody joined together?

C: Yes!

L: Wow, what great work in helping these people get connected. Okay, now we need Emily to explain why we did it. Why did we do that Emily?

Emily: Because you said to?

L: Well, I guess that's right, but when we do nice things for people it's also because we want them to know that Jesus loves them. Can you say to the people "Jesus loves you"?

Emily: Jesus loves you.

L: That was great, but, well, I wonder if everyone heard. Maybe we need all of the children to say that so the word gets out. Ready, "Jesus loves you" on three. One, two, three...

C: Jesus loves you!

L: That was super! And I bet it would be even better if the whole congregation joined in so we could tell the whole community. Ready? On three, one, two, three.

All: Jesus loves you!

L: That's right, and that's what we are called to do as we partner together in spreading the good news about Jesus Christ. We're to stand side by side, helping people with whatever needs they have, and then tell them why we did it and help them to know the love of God. Let's have a prayer and ask God to give us boldness in being show and tell Christians . . . *(prayer)*.

Brant D. Baker

Good Students!

Scripture: Proverbs 23:12

Season/Sunday: Back to school

Focus: God wants us to do our best to be good students.

Experience: A teacher will give the children some pointers on how to be good students.

Arrangements: Recruit a teacher (or a former teacher) in your congregation to be interviewed during the children's sermon, or better yet, invite one from a school that many of your church's children attend. An elementary school teacher is ideal, but any teacher from preschool to college will be able to give the children tips on how to be good students. Clue the teacher in ahead of time to the questions you will be asking. Consider bringing an apple as a simple thank you gift to present at the end of the sermon (use a clean cloth to give the apple a nice shine).

> **Leader:** Today, in honor of back to school, we have an honored guest (*call the teacher forward*). This is "Mr. Edwards," and he teaches third grade at Eisenhower Elementary, just up the street. Let's tell him good morning.
>
> **C:** Good morning, Mr. Edwards!
>
> **L:** There is a verse in the Bible that says, "Apply your mind to instruction and your ears to words of knowledge" (Proverbs 23:12). This means that God wants us to try very hard in school to be good students. God doesn't expect us to make perfect grades, but to apply our minds and do the best we can. That's what it means to be a good student. Let's ask Mr. Edwards for some advice on how to be a good student. What is one thing kids can do to be good students?

Teacher: *(Responds.)*

L: And what's another thing kids can do to be good students?

T: *(Responds.)*

L: And what's one more thing?

T: *(Responds.)*

L: Can you tell us a tiny bit about one of your best students from last year?

T: *(Responds.)*

L: Do you think these kids look like they will be good students this year?

T: Yes!

L: Let's ask the choir. Do you think these kids will be good students this year?

Choir: Yes!

L: Let's ask the congregation. Do you think these kids will be good students this year?

Congregation: Yes!

L: And now let's ask the kids. You look like good students to me. Do you think you will do well in school this year?

C: Yes!

L: Let's say a prayer thanking God for fine teachers and for good students . . . *(prayer)*. *(Hold the apple high in the air.)* And here is a very traditional teacher's gift to thank Mr. Edwards today *(present the apple to the teacher and accept the teacher's thanks)*.

Barbara Younger

Sweeter Than Honey

Scripture: Psalm 19:7-10

Season/Sunday: Any or Christian Education Sunday

Focus: The commandments are good, sweet, and desirable.

Experience: To associate the commandments/laws of God with something sweet.

Arrangements: Jar of honey (I prefer the one shaped like a bear) and a Bible with the passage marked. A handful of honey candies would make a nice giveaway at the end of the sermon.

Leader: Good morning. I was wondering, what is the sweetest thing you have ever eaten?

Children: Cookies. Cake. Chocolate candy.

L: Wow, those sound really tasty *(take out your honey jar)*. Have you ever eaten honey?

C: Yes! Now that's sweet! Yuck!

L: I like honey. It's the sweetest thing I have ever eaten *(eat a small spoonful)*. Mmm, that's good! That's very sweet. I can't think of anything sweeter. But the Bible says there is something sweeter than honey? Do you know what it is?

C: *(Various guesses.)*

L: Let me read to you from Psalm 19:7-10 *(read passage with special attention to verse 10. Read very slowly as if you can taste the words)*. Mmmmm—you can almost taste how good those words are, and how good it is to obey God's commandments. So, reading God's word and obeying God's commandments are even sweeter than the sweetest thing we know. Let's have a prayer and give thanks for God's sweet commandments . . . *(prayer). (Optional: candy giveaway.)*

Jeff L. Hutcheson

81

We're All a Part of God's Flock

Scripture: Luke 15:1-7

Season/Sunday: Any

Focus: God wants all of us to be his followers. We, in turn, should seek to include everyone in the flock of those who believe in Jesus.

Experience: The children will search for the lost sheep and hear about how God wants every one of us to be his followers and doesn't want a single soul to be lost.

Arrangements: Speak to one older child, prior to the service, who can stay in the pew and pretend to be the lost sheep. Have him or her sit near the back of the church and duck down behind the pew when the sermon starts. He or she should "Baa!" at the appointed time.

> **Leader:** Jesus hung out and ate with all kinds of people. Sometimes the church leaders of his day didn't approve of the people who he was hanging out with and they complained about it. Today we hear that the Jewish leaders didn't like the fact that Jesus was eating with people the leaders considered sinners. So Jesus told them a story. Did you ever hear the story of the lost sheep?
>
> **Children:** Yes!
>
> **L:** Who can remember what happened in the story of the lost sheep?
>
> **From the Pews:** Baa! Baa! Baa!
>
> **L:** What's that I hear? Why, it sounds like a sheep! I wonder where the sheep is? Where do you think it is?
>
> **C:** Out there!
>
> **From the Pews:** Baa! Baa! Baa!

L: Why don't we go look for the sheep? Which way do you think we should we go?

C: Over here! Over here! *(Children lead the leader around the church until they find the sheep. If they have trouble finding it, then the leader can help focus them in the correct direction.)* We found the sheep! We found her!

L: Look what we found! "Sarah" was our lost sheep! Now we can include her as part of the flock again. Just like the example in Jesus' story about the shepherd looking for his lost sheep, we don't want anyone to be left out either. What can we do to include people and bring them to church?

C: Invite other family members to come. Invite my friends. Invite my neighbors.

L: That's right! We can invite other people to join us in church so that together we celebrate the fact that God loves all of us! Let's say a prayer and give thanks that God loves us so much and doesn't want to lose even one sheep from the flock . . . *(prayer)*.

Susan M. Lang

Making a Baptism Gift

Scripture: Deuteronomy 4:9-10

Season/Sunday: Baby's baptism

Focus: The church helps babies grow to be Christians.

Experience: By making a baptism gift, the children will learn how the church has responsibility to help babies know God's love.

Arrangements: Purchase a square of fleece for a baby blanket (or some other item that may be completed as a gift). Cut fringes on two or three sides of the blanket, leaving enough space for the children to each cut at least one fringe during the service. Provide scissors to cut the fringes of the blanket. If most of your children are preschool, ask parents or other adults to accompany the children to the front to assist with this experience.

Leader: Good morning! This is a special day for a member of our church family. Today the pastor is going to baptize [has baptized] *(Name)*. Baptizing a baby holds a special meaning. It means that we recognize how God will be a part of this child throughout life. It also means that we, as a church family, will help the child to know God's love. What are some ways that we can show love?

Children: *(Various responses.)*

L: These are all good ways. I brought something today that we can make and give to the baby, which will also show God's love. Each of you will have a chance to cut one of the fringes on the blanket. As you finish cutting your fringe, I'd like for you to say, "We love you, *(Name)* and God loves you."

C: *(Various responses as each child cuts a fringe.)*

L: Thank you for helping to make this blanket *(if it isn't finished say, "I'll see that the blanket gets finished before we give it to [Name]."*) The baby will feel loved each time he or she uses it. You are helping to share God's love with this child. When you see *(Name)* here at church, be sure to stop and talk to him or her. Let's have a prayer. Will each of you take hold of the blanket as we pray?

Thank you, God, for *(Name)* and that he or she is now a part of our church family. We want *(Name)* to know that you love him or her and that he or she is a very special person. Amen. *(If the blanket is complete, present it to the baby.)*

Delia Halverson

Celebrating Communion Around the World

Scripture: Galatians 3:26-28

Season/Sunday: World Communion Sunday

Focus: One of the things we affirm as Christians is that all of the various churches, when taken together, are the one body of Jesus Christ. On World Communion Sunday we celebrate that oneness. We know Christians around the world share the Lord's Supper on this same day, transcending geographical and even political barriers.

Experience: To become the globe, with representatives from cities around the world.

Arrangements: There are at least two ways this sermon could be done. The first is as presented below, with the children circling around the table and representing the global community as they pass the cup and say the brief prayer. For this version you will need a list of cities in different time zones. Another option would be to visit an adult Sunday school class before church and hand out eighteen copies of the list of cities, assigning one city per person. Their instructions would be to stand up after a signal from you, wherever they are in the sanctuary, and read the names of their assigned city in the order it appears. The children could respond as a group with the brief prayer after each city had been called out. In this case people standing up all over the congregation would represent the globe.

> **Leader:** Good morning! Let's make a big circle around the Communion Table, and let's make it big enough so there is room for everybody, so that we're all in a circle around the table. Today is World Communion Sunday, which is a very special day because it means that all over the world, all around the world *(motion to the circle as if it were the world)*, Christians are celebrating communion. What if we did something to re-

mind ourselves that every hour during this day, somewhere somebody is celebrating the Lord's Supper? How about if I give someone the cup and then read the name of a city somewhere in the world, saying, "In such and such a city, " and then have the person holding the cup say, "We thank God for sending Jesus Christ." In a way, each one of us will become a representative of the Christians in that city. *(Turn to first child.)* Will you take the cup? Thanks. Okay, here we go:
In Mexico City, Mexico . . .

Child: We thank God for sending Jesus Christ.

L: Good! Would you like to hold it next? I need some volunteers! Thank you. In Los Angeles . . .

Child: We thank God for sending Jesus Christ *(repeat for all cities).*

L: Vancouver, Canada
Papatee, Tahiti
Honolulu
Pago Pago, Samoa
Christchurch, New Zealand
Sidney, Australia
Tokyo, Japan
Seoul, Korea
Saigon, Viet Nam
Bangkok, Thailand
Kabul, Afghanistan
Tehran, Iran
Moscow, Russia
Rome, Italy
London, England
Your hometown

Great! You did a good job and reminded us that all around the world today Christians are celebrating God sending Jesus Christ. Let's all hold hands and have a prayer thanking God for giving us such a good way to remember Jesus through Communion, and for all the Christians all over the world today who are our brothers and sisters . . . *(prayer).*

Brant D. Baker

I'm Sad

Scripture: Psalm 42:5-6a

Season/Sunday: Any

Focus: Children will hear that it is okay to be sad sometimes and should know that God is with us even in those sad times.

Experience: Children will try different things to cheer up the leader.

Arrangements: Arrange for another person to take the role of the helper. Collect the props mentioned in the sermon (a can of soda, a chocolate bar, and a stuffed animal) and recruit volunteers to offer each one on cue. Finally, ask the accompanist to be prepared to play a song that the children will know such as "Twinkle, Twinkle Little Star" or "Jesus Loves Me."

Helper:	Good morning "Ms. Karen," are you okay?
Leader:	*(Looking sad.)* No, not really. I'm kind of bummed out this morning.
H:	You *are* looking a little sad this morning. Is there something we can do to make you feel better?
L:	Oh, I don't know. Sometimes a soda helps. I'd probably feel better if I had one of those.
H:	Gosh, I don't have a soda. *(Looking at the children and congregation.)* Does anyone have a soda?
Volunteer 1:	I just happen to have one here in my robe—always good to have an extra soda in your pocket in case you get thirsty!
H:	Wow, thanks "Pastor Geoffrey." Here you go Ms. Karen. Do you feel better now? Do you want to have a drink?
L:	No. I don't really feel any better. I guess that wasn't what I needed.

H: Well, okay. Is there anything else we can do to make you feel better?

L: *(Pause and sigh.)* Well sometimes, chocolate helps.

H: Chocolate? Okay, does anybody have any chocolate?

Volunteer 2: I do!

H: There we go. How do you feel now, Ms. Karen?

L: Not much better. It didn't really help.

H: What would help?

L: Well, a stuffed animal usually helps.

H: A stuffed animal. Well, can anyone help with that?

Volunteer 3: Just happen to have one!

H: Hooray! This is bound to do the trick. There you go, Ms. Karen. Hug on that. Now how do you feel?

L: *(Sighing heavily.)* Still not good.

H: What else can we do?

L: You know, sometimes when people sing to me I feel better. I really like "Twinkle, Twinkle Little Star."

H: *(To the children.)* Can you help me sing Ms. Karen a song?

Children: *(Sing.)*

H: Now how do you feel?

L: *(Hugging the stuffed animal.)* Still sad.

H: I have to tell you something, Ms. Karen: I don't think any of this stuff is going to make you feel better. Sometimes we're just sad, and that's okay. In fact, the Bible even has some prayers for sad times called Psalms of Lament. One of my favorites is verse 5 from Psalm 42. It says, "Why are you cast down, O my soul, and why are you disquieted within me? Hope in God; for I shall again praise him, my help and my God." Sometimes life is hard and it's good to know that we can pray and God will help us through those sad times.

L: Well, I think I'll try that. Will you all pray with me? Dear God, please be with us when we feel bad or sad, and thank you for understanding when we are down. Amen.

Karen Evans

Knee-Mail!

Scripture: Ephesians 3:14 (NIV)

Season/Sunday: Any

Focus: This sermon focuses on the act of kneeling in prayer.

Experience: Children will experience what for them is often a very simple task, that of kneeling to say our prayers. While they are not yet cognizant of the humility expressed by kneeling, the experience gives them both the idea and the chance to practice this important posture before God.

Arrangements: None needed

Leader: Welcome everyone! I have a question for you: what position are you in when you pray? By "position" I mean how your body is placed when you pray. For instance do you sit when you pray?

Children: Yes. I am lying down when I pray. Me too.

L: Okay, let's practice those. Some of the time we sit when we pray, so let's all sit and fold our hands like we are praying.

C: *(Children all sit.)*

L: Good. And some of you said you are lying down when you pray; let's do that.

C: *(Giggles. Children lie flat.)*

L: Good. Are there other ways? Do you ever see people pray *(start to stand up).*

C: Standing up!

L: Yes, that is a good way to pray. Let's do that.

C: *(Children stand.)* How about walking?

L: Yes, we know we can pray when we walk. Good! Well, today we have a verse from the Bible that talks about another posture for prayer. Let's say the verse together, with you echoing me, "For this reason *(pause)*, I kneel before the Father" *(pause)* and I pray *(pause)*.

Let's practice that position *(get on knees)*. Did you know that this is one of the best positions of all for prayer?

C: No.

L: It really is. God likes us to get on our knees when we pray, if we can, because it shows respect and love for God. Hey! Since we're on our knees right now, why don't we say a prayer and thank God we can pray in so many different ways . . . *(prayer)*.

Bob Sharman

Happy to Give

Scripture: 2 Corinthians 9:6-8 (CEV)

Season/Sunday: Stewardship

Focus: Based on Paul's instruction to make up our own minds about giving, the children will respond to different giving scenarios with a focus on their feelings. They will learn that God loves those who give with a happy heart.

Experience: The sermon intersperses the scripture with objects, role-playing, and question/response. The concepts of planting and harvest are introduced using seeds and ears of corn, and then linked to the joy of giving. Through questions and the role-playing of two volunteers, the children can contrast grumpy giving with happy giving.

Arrangements: You will need a packet of corn seeds and four ears of corn. Check the packet for a seed count, as you will need this information for the sermon. Remove one seed to use in the opening of the sermon. You will also need two young volunteers of elementary school age or older to demonstrate grumpy giving and happy giving. Recruit them ahead of time and explain that Child One will need to show grumpiness in tone of voice and actions, as well as in words, such as, "Take this stupid corn!" Child Two will receive the corn with a hurt expression. Next, Child Two, now holding the corn, will illustrate happy giving with voice and actions, saying something like, "This corn is so good, I want to share some with you!"

> **Leader:** Look at this! *(Hold up corn seed.)* This seed is a dried kernel of corn. If it is planted in good soil in the springtime and if it gets a nice mix of rain and sunshine, then the seed will grow into a cornstalk. One

cornstalk makes two to four ears of corn *(hold up four ears of corn).* How many ears do you count?

Children: Four!

L: Right! Would it be fun to grow a cornstalk, pick the corn, and then eat it with your family?

C: Yes!

L: What's this? *(Hold up a packet of corn seeds.)*

C: Bag of corn, more corn seeds.

L: There are *(number)* seeds in this packet. That means we could grow *(number of seeds)* cornstalks to harvest *(number of seeds multiplied by four)* ears of corn. If you could choose to plant one seed or a whole packet of seeds, what would you do?

C: Plant a whole packet!

L: In chapter 9 of Second Corinthians, the scripture says, "A few seeds make a small harvest, but a lot of seeds make a big harvest." If we had a big harvest of delicious ears of corn, would you feel happy or grumpy?

C: Happy!

L: Okay! If you invited everyone here at church to a corn roasting party at your house to eat the big harvest, would you be happy or grumpy?

C: Happy!

L: Me too! Or, if you shared your harvest of corn with children who don't have enough to eat, would you be happy or grumpy?

C: Happy!

L: Good! In a letter to the Corinthian church, the Apostle Paul writes that God wants us to feel happy when we give to others. Can you think of a time when you were happy to give?

C: Pennies for hunger. Toys for the Christmas angel tree. Making a gift for Grandma.

L: Paul says that each of us must make up our own minds about how much we give. He tells us not to feel forced to give. Can you remember a time when you were grumpy about giving or sharing?

C: Mom made me share a new toy. I shared a snack with a kid who ate it all.

L: Feeling grumpy takes the happiness out of giving *(introduce volunteers; hand Child One, "Johnny," the ears of corn)*. Watch Johnny carefully to see if he is grumpy or happy to give *(Johnny acts grumpy while giving ears of corn to Child Two, "Susie")*. What kind of giving was that?

C: Grumpy!

L: Do you think Susie felt happy to get the gift?

C: Not really.

L: Let's watch our volunteers again. *(Susie, now holding corn, kindly gives corn to Johnny)*. Was that grumpy or happy giving?

C: Happy!

L: Do you think Johnny felt happy to get the gift? *(Take corn and let volunteers sit.)*

C: Yes!

L: You can see that when you give with a happy heart, your gift is received with happiness. Paul tells us that God loves people who love to give. Say that with me!

C: God loves people who love to give.

L: And if we give a lot to others, God will love what we are doing and help us! Let's have a prayer and give thanks that we can plant many seeds, give with happy hearts, and enjoy God's love . . . *(prayer)*.

Lisa Flinn

Plus Nine

Scripture: Leviticus 27:30; Deuteronomy 14:22

Season/Sunday: Stewardship

Focus: Help children recognize a tithe as our way of giving thanks to God.

Experience: The children will experience receiving and giving back.

Arrangements: Have a basket with ten lollypops for each child. Arrange for an usher to come forward at appropriate time with an offering plate.

Leader: Good morning! What do you suppose is in my basket?
Children: *(Various responses.)*
    L: I have something special that will make you happy. Do you want to see?
    C: Lollypops! Can I have one?
    L: Let me give each of you ten of the items in my basket. Don't eat them now. Wait until your parents tell you it's okay. *(Count out ten lollypops for each child. If you have a large group and time is limited, arrange ahead of time for another adult to help you.)*
    L: You know, I heard about a child who is very sad. *(Tell the children about another child who is ill or sad for some reason, a child that can be a mission project. Or you may speak of homeless children who are without homes and who are sad.)*
    L: Do you suppose lollypops would cheer him or her up?
    C: *(Various responses.)*
    L: Let's see. You each have ten lollypops. Do you suppose that each of you could give up one of your

lollypops to make a child happy? *(Have an usher pass around an offering plate for each child to put a lolly-pop in. If a child does not want to do so, allow him or her to make that choice. Thank the usher for help-ing.)*

L: We will see that the lollypop gifts are given to *(Name)* so that he or she can be happier. Now let me ask you: did you have any lollypops when you came up here this morning?

C: No.

L: This is the way that God is with us, and how we should act for God. God gives us an ability to make money, and we give back to God one out of every ten dollars we make. This is what is called a tithe, or one-tenth. We give that to the church so that the church can do good things in God's name. There is a verse in the Bible that tells us to do this *(read Leviticus 27:30 or Deuteronomy 14:22)*. Let's have a prayer and give thanks that we can help out by giving our tithe . . . *(prayer)*.

Delia Halverson

Doxology

Scripture: Psalm 113:1

Season/Sunday: Any, or a Sunday near Thanksgiving

Focus: To learn about praising God as a constant way of life.

Experience: To interact with an idea called *Doxology*. A sermon of the same name, given by the great preacher Fred Craddock, was the inspiration for this children's sermon version.

Arrangements: None are needed, but you might want to have the church musician ready to lead the singing of the Doxology.

Leader: Good morning. Let me introduce you to an idea *(look down the aisle)*. Let's see if I can get the idea to come up front *(motion, wave, and call the idea up front like you would a pet, and smile after it reaches you)*. That sure is a nice idea. It feels good when I stand next to it.

Children: *(Giggling and staring like you are crazy.)*

L: *(Pretend you are picking up a small dog and hold it in your arms.)* This idea first came to me a while back. I was tired one evening. It had been a long day, and I was resting outside on the front step. That's when the idea came to me. It wasn't my idea, but we played and talked until it got dark and time for everyone to go home. I don't know where it lives but it sure was fun to be around. Well, this got to be a regular end of my day. Each night after a long day I'd go out on the porch, and the idea would wander up. Even Gizmo, our dog, liked the idea. We would play and we would laugh, and I just kept hoping that this idea had a home that it belonged to. So one weekend I went around the neighborhood, and knocked on all the doors, asking if the idea belonged to them. Everyone loved the idea, but no one knew where it belonged.

Well, I just couldn't let it wander the streets. So I took it home, and Gizmo and I asked Sherri if the idea could move in with us. You know what she said?

C: What?

L: She took one look at the idea, smiled and said, "Absolutely, it can live here." So we made a place for the idea in our home. Still, we needed to give it a name. This idea was part of the family now. It needed a name. So we thought and we thought, and we named it Doxology.

C: That's a funny name.

L: Well, it may sound unusual but it is a name that fits the idea perfectly. Let's say it together.

L&C: Doxology.

L: I take Doxology with me everywhere I go. Doxology loves to go with me when I'm riding in the car, when I go to the hospital to visit people, even when I go to the grocery store. It doesn't matter where I go, as long as Doxology is with me, the days seem brighter and the world seems more alive and splendid. Doxology loves to come to worship. That's right: Doxology loves to come to worship! Do you know why? Do you know what doxology is?

C: No.

L: Doxology is praise to God. Doxology is us saying thank-you to God and praising God for all the wonderful things God does for us and for how great and good God is. The Bible says that all people everywhere are to "praise the Lord." There's even a song we sing in church that you have probably heard but just never thought about what it was. Let's ask the congregation to stand and we'll all sing the Doxology *(invite the congregation to stand and sing the Doxology)*.

Don't forget to take Doxology with you today when you leave. Doxology loves to worship, but it's not meant to just stay here and be visited once a week. Doxology loves to travel everywhere and be with you all the time. Let's have a prayer and give thanks that it feels so good when we give God thanks . . . *(praise)*.

Jeff L. Hutcheson

The Thankful Game

Scripture: Psalm 92:1

Season/Sunday: Thanksgiving

Focus: This sermon helps us think about the many things we have to be thankful for in God's world.

Experience: Children will learn a fun game for Thanksgiving. The leader will name a category. Children and others in the congregation will call out a favorite in that category.

Arrangements: None

Leader: I am so thankful that all of you are here today! And I'm thankful that we can worship in our lovely church. And I'm thankful for one of my favorite holidays. Which holiday do you think I am especially thankful for today?

Children: Thanksgiving.

L: Are you thankful for Thanksgiving?

C: Yes.

L: Can you tell me some of the reasons you are thankful for Thanksgiving?

C: I like turkey. I like Grandma's pies. My cousins are coming to my house.

L: I'm thankful for fun games, too. Do you like to play games?

C: Yes.

L: In honor of Thanksgiving and all the wonderful things God has given us to be thankful for, I'm going to teach you how to play the Thankful Game. Some families like to play this game on Thanksgiving Day, while dinner is cooking or when they are enjoying the delicious meal. Are you ready?

C: Yes.

L: First, let's name foods we are thankful for. I'm thankful for *(name a favorite food)*. How about you?

C: *(Children name foods. The congregation can be invited to call out favorites throughout the sermon as well.)*

L: Now, let's all name an animal we are thankful for. I'm thankful for *(name a favorite animal)*. How about you?

C: *(Children name animals.)*

L: Next, let's name a color we are thankful for. I'm thankful for *(name a favorite color)*. How about you?

C: *(Children name colors.)*

L: Here's our last category for today. Let's name an activity we are thankful for. I'm thankful for *(name an activity)*.

C: *(Children name activities.)*

L: Thanks for playing the Thankful Game. You did a great job. I hope you will play the game this Thanksgiving at your house. You can have fun making up lots of new categories. We have so much to be thankful for and as the Bible tells us, "It is good to give thanks to the LORD." Let's say a prayer together thanking God . . . *(prayer)*.

Barbara Younger

Bethlehem Bakery: Overview and Recipe

"Bethlehem Bakery: House of Bread" is a six-part children's sermon series for Advent, Christmas, and Epiphany. The series connects the process of making bread with the message of these seasons—that God took steps in preparing the world to receive Jesus, the Bread of Life, born in Bethlehem, the "house of bread." Just as bread making involves preparing a recipe, sifting the ingredients, blending the mixture, working the dough, baking the loaf, and sharing the results, so also God's process involved preparing a place, sending the prophets, arranging the plans, empowering the people, giving the gift, and sharing the story.

The leader plays the role of a baker and could come each week dressed in an apron and chef's hat to lead the children in the process of preparing to make bread and learning about the bread of life.

RECIPE FOR OVERNIGHT BREAD DOUGH

Ingredients
2 packages dry yeast
2½ cups warm water
¾ cup melted/soft shortening, or oil
¾ cup sugar
2 eggs, well beaten
8 to 8½ cups flour
2½ teaspoons salt

Instructions
Soften yeast in warm water; add shortening, sugar, eggs, salt, and 4 cups flour. Stir together; beat until smooth. Stir in the remaining flour one cup at a time, making a soft dough. Work last cup of flour in by hand, on a board, if necessary. Place in greased bowl; lightly grease surface and cover. Store in refrigerator overnight, or until needed, punching down occasionally. Shape into loaves or rolls; let rise until doubled in size. Bake at 400 degrees for 15 to 20 minutes for rolls, or until well browned for loaves.

Bethlehem Bakery: Preparing the Recipe

Scripture: Micah 5:2-5a

Season/Sunday: First Sunday of Advent

Focus: Bread is a symbol that can help us understand God's plan to provide a Savior who would be born in Bethlehem, the "house of bread."

Experience: The children will pretend to put on their baker's hats and aprons, review a recipe for bread, and receive an Advent bookmark to take home as a reminder of God's recipe for salvation.

Arrangements: The leader could play the part of the baker who specializes in bread making. He or she could wear a baker's hat and apron. You will need an illustrated recipe for yeast bread marked in a cookbook with one of the Advent bookmarks, and a Bible marked with another bookmark. Leaders can make simple bookmarks with the words *Bethlehem: House of Bread*, and include the verses from Micah 5 and clip art of the city of Bethlehem. On the other side add a yeast bread recipe if desired.

> **Leader:** Welcome to our Bethlehem Bakery where we'll be preparing bread for a special occasion! Who knows what special time is coming?
>
> **Children:** Christmas!
>
> **L:** Well, yes, but before Christmas is the four-week season of preparing called Advent. In Advent, we get our hearts and minds ready to reexperience the birth of our Savior. Who is that, and where was our Savior born? Do you know?
>
> **C:** Jesus! He was born in Bethlehem!
>
> **L:** Right! And do you know that Bethlehem means "house of bread" in the Hebrew language? God chose

to send Jesus to Earth in a little town whose name represents what human beings need to live—bread! Even more amazing, Jesus, our Savior, is also called the "bread of life"! So during Advent, as we think about how God prepared the "house of bread" to be the birthplace of the bread of life, we are going to pretend that we are all bakers of bread! Can you put on your pretend apron and your tall baker's hat? *(Guide children in a pantomime.)*

C: *(Pretend to put on aprons and baker's hats.)*

L: Now, what is the first thing a baker must do to get ready to bake bread?

C: Wash your hands! Light the oven! Get the flour!

L: Those are all good suggestions. But even before we begin to get out the ingredients, we need a recipe that will explain the process and guide us as we prepare the dough. *(Open the recipe book to the bookmarked page and show the picture of the bread and the instructions for making the bread.)* To create delicious bread we must begin with a recipe. God began with a recipe, too *(open Bible to bookmarked passage)*. In fact, many, many years before Jesus was born, God's prophets wrote the recipe, in Micah 5:2, of where the bread of life would be born—in Bethlehem, the "house of bread."

Advent is a time for us to remember that God had a plan for saving the world, a recipe that took time to get ready. Let's say an echo-prayer together, giving thanks for God's good plan *(invite the children to repeat each line of the prayer, pausing at appropriate intervals.)* Dear God *(pause)*, thank you for the plan to send us a Savior *(pause)*. Help us share your plan with others *(pause)* so that everyone may have the Bread of Life *(pause)*. Amen.

That was great, and I have a bookmark for you to take home as a reminder of Advent and of God's recipe for saving the world. Be sure to come back next week for the second Sunday of Advent at the Bethlehem Bakery!

Ann Liechty and Phyllis Wezeman

Bethlehem Bakery: Sifting the Ingredients

Scripture: Isaiah 7:14

Season/Sunday: Second Sunday of Advent

Focus: The varied ingredients for making bread can symbolize the many prophecies and people that God assembled in order to produce the desired outcome, a Savior who would be born in Bethlehem, the "house of bread."

Experience: The children will pretend to put on their baker's hats and aprons, to follow the recipe for bread, and to sift the dry ingredients that must be assembled in order to create the dough, just like God assembled all the right ingredients prior to Jesus' birth.

Arrangements: The leader wears a baker's hat and apron and plays the part of the baker who has assembled all the dry ingredients for sifting. The baker could provide small, clear glass or plastic containers filled with the measured dry ingredients. If feasible, the Baker could actually demonstrate the sifting process using a large sifter and a mixing bowl. The Overnight Refrigerator Dough recipe (see p. 101) calls for these dry ingredients: 2 packages dry yeast, ¾ cup sugar, 8 to 8½ cups flour, and 2½ teaspoons salt. The instructions in the recipe are to sift the flour with the salt. The other ingredients will not be added until Week Three.

> **Leader:** Welcome back to the Bethlehem Bakery! Are you ready to get started with our recipe for making bread? Today I brought the first of our ingredients. But before we begin, what does the baker need to do? (*Pantomime any appropriate actions that the children suggest.*)
>
> **Children:** Put on our aprons! Put on our hats! Wash our hands! Follow the recipe!

104

L: That's right! Next we need our ingredients. Good
bread begins with good ingredients! Here are some of
the ingredients that our recipe calls for. Does anyone
know what this one is *(show flour)*?

C: *(Make guesses.)*

L: This is flour, which is the main ingredient in bread.
This flour comes from ground wheat, but you could
also have flour from barley or any other kind of
grain. Okay, what are these? *(Show sugar and salt.)*

C: *(Make guesses.)*

L: This one is salt, which we use to preserve and flavor
our food, and the other one is sugar. Does anyone
know what this is? *(show yeast.)*

C: *(Make guesses.)*

L: This is called yeast. Yeast is a living organism that
eats the sugar and forms carbon dioxide gas, which
then causes bread to expand and rise. Okay, now, before we can stir the ingredients together, we need to
do some sifting *(hold up the sifter)*. The sifter sepa-
rates the larger, heavier particles found in the flour
and breaks up any lumps. If we sift our dry ingredients, then our bread will rise higher and be lighter in
texture. Help me while I sift the flour *(guide the children to pantomime the sifting motion. If the leader is
actually sifting, use only one cup of the flour.)*

L: Wow! It takes a long time to sift everything, doesn't it?

C: Yes!

L: Last week, as Advent began, we remembered that
God took a long time to put together the recipe for
sending the Savior. This Sunday, we begin the second
week of Advent, and we find that God's recipe still re-
quires more gathering of the ingredients. There is a
lot to sift through in the story of Jesus' birth. God
sent many prophets to tell of Jesus' coming. Have you
ever heard any of the prophets' names?

C: Moses? Noah?

L: Well, one of the most famous prophets was named
Isaiah. Many, many years before Jesus was born,
Isaiah wrote about a young woman who would give
birth to the Savior. But even before Isaiah, came God's

promise to a woman you may have heard about—her name was Eve. Who was she?

C: Adam's wife! She ate an apple!

L: Even though Adam and Eve chose to disobey God, God still loved them. God promised that through Eve's descendents, humans would receive a Savior. That story goes all the way back to the beginning of humans on the Earth. Wow! God's been sifting out this recipe for a long time! Next week, on the Third Sunday of Advent, we will finally be ready to mix up the dough for our Bethlehem Bakery! Let's take off our baker's hats and our aprons.

C: *(Pretend to remove aprons and hats.)*

L: And say an echo prayer asking God to help us sift through all the details of the plan for Jesus' birth. Let's pray:

Dear God *(pause for echo)*, thank you for putting everything in place *(pause)* to fulfill your plan for the Earth *(pause)*. Help us take the time to sift through the details *(pause)* and appreciate each ingredient in the story of Jesus' birth *(pause)*. Amen.

Ann Liechty and Phyllis Wezeman

Bethlehem Bakery: Blending the Mixture

Scripture: Isaiah 40:3

Season/Sunday: Third Sunday of Advent

Focus: The process of blending the mixture of ingredients to create the dough represents the process God used to prepare the way for a Savior who would be born in Bethlehem, the "house of bread."

Experience: The children will pretend to put on their baker's hats and aprons, to follow the recipe for bread, and to stir the ingredients that create the dough, just like God blended prophecy and people to prepare the way for Jesus' birth.

Arrangements: The leader wears a baker's hat and apron and plays the part of the baker who, today, mixes the dry and wet ingredients to create the dough. The baker could demonstrate mixing all of the ingredients. If feasible, the baker could allow the participants to contribute the different ingredients by dumping each item from its container into a large mixing bowl. The Overnight Refrigerator Dough recipe calls for last week's sifted, dry ingredients to be mixed with two packages of dry yeast dissolved in 2½ cups of warm water, which should be prepared just prior to the demonstration. The rest of the recipe calls for ¾ cup melted/soft shortening, or oil; and 2 eggs well beaten. Divide the sifted, dry ingredients in half and place 4 cups of the flour mixture in a large bowl in order to mix them with the liquids. Stir in the remaining flour gradually, after the liquids have been blended thoroughly.

> **Leader:** Here we are for the third time at our Bethlehem Bakery! As we get closer to Christmas, things get more exciting! Today we are going to mix all the ingredients together and make the dough! Have you ever

made a lot of dough? Not money! Bread dough! It
takes a lot of stirring to blend together all of these ingredients. So let's get started! What does the baker
need to do? *(Pantomime any appropriate actions that
the children suggest.)*

Children: Put on our aprons! Put on our hats! Wash our hands!
Find the recipe! Sift the ingredients!

L: Last week we sifted the flour and salt together and
collected all our dry ingredients. Today we need to
blend dry and wet ingredients together. Let's start by
stirring together all the dry ingredients. Chefs often
advise us to stir in a figure-eight motion. Let's practice
stirring the ingredients. *(Using a spoon, demonstrate
a figure-eight motion in the air and encourage the
children to pantomime until they master the motion.)*

C: *(Pantomime the figure-eight motion.)*

L: If we make a sideways figure eight *(demonstrate
again)*, we are creating the symbol for infinity. Infinity
is the forever place where God dwells. Maybe that is
why God is so patient and spent so many years getting
all the right ingredients together to send Jesus to earth!

C: *(Children pantomime infinity symbol.)*

L: Now that the dry ingredients are all blended, we must
prepare to add the liquid to our mixture. We do that
by making a small well, or hollow, in half of the dry
ingredients *(demonstrate scooping out a well to receive the liquids)*. And just like we prepare a place for
the liquids, God prepared the way for Jesus to come
to earth. God promised, through the prophet Isaiah,
that someone would be sent to prepare the way for
the Messiah. Do you know his name?

C: Santa Claus? John the Baptist?

L: That someone was John the Baptist, Jesus' cousin
who was born to Zechariah and Elizabeth in their old
age just as the angel had promised—quite a miracle!
As we combine all the different liquids we must stir!
*(If feasible, have children add oil, sugar, and beaten
eggs to the yeast and water mixture, or add premixed
liquids all at once. Have the children repeat the figure
eight motion.)*

C: *(Help "stir" the ingredients by pantomiming the figure eight motion.)*

L: The dough must have just the right texture before we let it rest and rise, so we keep adding flour and blending until the dough feels just right. This blending takes a lot of time and energy! No wonder God chose to send the Messiah to be born in Bethlehem, the "house of bread"! Bakers understand the effort and patience God needed to provide the world with the Bread of Life. Let's take off our bakers' hats and aprons.

C: *(Pretend to remove aprons and hats.)*

L: And ask God to give us the patience, to keep working to blend love and peace into our daily lives, with an echo prayer. Ready?

Dear God *(pause for echo)*, thank you for sending special messengers to prepare the way for Jesus *(pause)*. Help us work together *(pause)* to prepare the way for his birth in our lives *(pause)* and in our world *(pause)*. Amen.

Ann Liechty and Phyllis Wezeman

Bethlehem Bakery: Working the Dough

Scripture: Luke 2:1-5

Season/Sunday: Fourth Sunday of Advent

Focus: The process of working the dough—kneading, shaping, and rising—reminds us that Mary and Joseph's contribution required both effort and trust as they cooperated with God's plan for a Savior who would be born in Bethlehem, the "house of bread."

Experience: The children will pretend to put on their baker's hats and aprons, to follow the recipe for bread, to stir the ingredients that create the dough, and to knead and shape the bread dough similar to how God worked through Mary and Joseph to prepare the way for Jesus' birth.

Arrangements: The leader wears a baker's hat and apron and plays the part of the baker who works the dough to knead, shape, and let it rise. The baker could demonstrate kneading and shaping the bread dough. If feasible, the baker could allow the participants to help knead and shape the loaves for rising. The dough must be prepared in advance to be ready to be worked by the children.

> **Leader:** Here we are for the fourth week at our Bethlehem Bakery! Our dough is almost ready to become bread. Yum! When we taste the fresh bread, all of our work will seem worth it. However, we have one more step to complete the process—just like we have this last Sunday of Advent before Christmas finally arrives. What does the baker need to do? *(Pantomime any appropriate actions that the children suggest.)*
>
> **Children:** Put on our aprons! Put on our hats! Wash our hands! Find the recipe! Sift the ingredients! Stir the mixture!

L: We have read the recipe, collected the ingredients, sifted the flour, and stirred the mixture. Now what do we need? We need to knead the bread! Get it? Kneading is the word for what we do next. We must work or knead the mixture with our hands to smooth out the texture, work out the air bubbles from the yeast, and shape our dough into a loaf so that it can double in size before we bake it. Kneading is actually the most important part of the bread making process. First, we flour the breadboard and our hands so the dough won't stick *(have the children pantomime this activity.)*

C: *(Pantomime flouring their hands.)*

L: Let me show you how to knead or work the dough. Make fists and push on the dough. Press the dough down and forward, then fold it and press in again.

C: *(Pantomime kneading imaginary dough.)*

L: It takes at least ten minutes of kneading to prepare the dough for baking. The more we press and push, fold and shape, and press again, the more elastic the dough becomes. If we knead the bread long enough, we should be able to stretch the mixture without it breaking. Kneading is a lot of work! But all the pushing and punching is what makes the bread good. *(Children continue to pretend to knead.)* Bread kneading can remind us that some events in life press in and stretch us nearly to the breaking point. But those pressing problems might be an important part of life's process that turns out to be good. When Caesar Augustus demanded that everyone return to their hometowns to be counted and taxed, Joseph and Mary made the difficult journey to Bethlehem. Mary was almost ready to have her baby. I'd guess that they felt like life was really pressing in on them! But Joseph and Mary were willing to obey God. They trusted God's plan. Their effort and trust resulted in the gift of a savior, the Bread of Life, born as God promised in Bethlehem, the "house of bread." How wonderful that God sent us exactly what we need at Christmas! Or is it exactly what we "knead" *(make kneading motion)*? Let's take off our bakers' hats.

C: *(Pretend to remove aprons and hats.)*

L: And thank God for giving us the faith we need so that in difficult times we may stretch, but not break. Let's pray:

Dear God *(pause for echo)*, thank you for the faithfulness of Mary and Joseph *(pause)*. Help us trust you always *(pause)*, just as they did on their journey to Bethlehem *(pause)*. Amen.

Ann Liechty and Phyllis Wezeman

Bethlehem Bakery: Baking the Loaf

Scripture: Luke 2:6-20

Season/Sunday: Christmas Sunday or Christmas Day

Focus: The baked loaf of bread invites us to enjoy God's gift of the Bread of Life, a Savior who is born in Bethlehem, the "house of bread."

Experience: The children will pretend to put on their baker's hats and aprons, and will pantomime a review of the bread-baking process—following the recipe, stirring the ingredients, and kneading and shaping the dough—so that they can celebrate the results of their efforts and relate their celebration to God's process of bringing Jesus to earth.

Arrangements: The leader wears a baker's hat and apron and plays the part of the baker who produces the bread, fresh from the oven. The baker could bring a warm loaf on a breadboard and reveal it to the children. If feasible (and hopefully it will be after all the hard work the children have put in!) the baker could allow the participants to taste a slice of the warm bread (be sensitive to concerns about possible wheat allergies). The bread must be baked in advance for the children to eat. You might want to have Luke 2:10 marked in a Bible for the volunteer reader.

Leader: Welcome to the Bethlehem Bakery on this special day that we have been waiting for, for so long! Our joy is complete today because we celebrate that Jesus is born! It has been a long process to get from God's first promise of the Messiah to the actual moment of the Savior's birth. We have remembered this process by comparing the preparation of Advent to the steps in making bread. What did we have to do to get ready for today? *(Pantomime any appropriate actions that the children suggest.)*

Children: Put on our aprons! Put on our hats! Wash our hands! Find the recipe! Sift the ingredients! Stir the mixture! Knead the dough! Shape the loaf!

  L: Whew! We've had a lot of steps to complete in order to reach our celebration today. Has it been worth the wait? *(Reveal the baked bread.)* I think so! Can you catch the smell of freshly baked bread this morning? Mmmmmm!

  C: Yum! Can we have some?

  L: Of course you may have a share in the bread because you helped to make this loaf! What about those here this morning who didn't help stir the ingredients or knead the dough? Should they get some of this bread too? Some of you might say, "Yes," and some of you might say, "No!"

  C: Yes! No! Maybe!

  L: Let's think about what our baking of the bread symbolizes. Each step of the bread making process in Advent has been designed to remind us of God's steps in preparing to send Jesus, the Bread of Life. Today—on Christmas—we celebrate that God's gift is complete, just like our loaf of bread. When the angels appeared to the shepherds in Bethlehem, what were the words they sang?

  C: *(Have a reader look in a Bible for Luke 2:10.)* "But the angel said to them, 'Do not be afraid; for see—I am bringing you good news of great joy for all the people.'"

  L: Exactly! God's joyous gift of Jesus was for everyone. After the shepherds went to see the baby the angels told them about, they also shared the story of the Messiah with everyone! So, our bread that symbolizes Jesus, the Bread of Life, is meant for everyone to share, not just the bakers. Let's have a prayer and give thanks to God for our bread and for this Christmas Day when we remember that Jesus, the Bread of Life, was born in Bethlehem, the "house of bread."

Dear God *(pause for echo)*, we give thanks that you sent us Jesus on Christmas Day *(pause)*. Help us always remember *(pause)* that your joyous gift is for everyone *(pause)*! Amen.

L: *(Share the bread with the group.)*

Anna Liechty and Phyllis Wezeman

Bethlehem Bakery: Sharing the Bread

Scripture: Matthew 2:10-11

Season/Sunday: Epiphany (or the Sunday after Christmas Sunday)

Focus: The wide assortment of breads from around the world reminds us that all people everywhere are offered God's gift of Jesus, who is the Bread of Life, a Savior born in Bethlehem, the "house of bread."

Experience: The children will pretend to put on their baker's hats and aprons, and will pantomime a review of the bread-baking process—following the recipe, stirring the ingredients, kneading and shaping the dough, and slicing the bread to eat—so that they can appreciate that bread is a staple of life for the world, just as God's gift of Jesus provides eternal life for the world.

Arrangements: The leader wears a baker's hat and apron and plays the part of the baker who displays a variety of breads such as corn, rye, and wheat. The baker *could* produce a basket of fresh breads and, if feasible, could allow the participants to taste the various types of bread.

Leader: Welcome, once again, to the Bethlehem Bakery! Did you think we were finished because Christmas has come and gone? Have you given up eating bread?

Children: No!

L: Of course, you are still getting hungry every day. People have hunger in common. All people get hungry every day and need food. Can you guess what is the most common food that people around the world eat?

C: Bread!

L: Yes! Here are some different kinds of breads found around the world (*reveal the different breads in the basket.*) Notice that the breads all have different colors and textures. They may look different than the bread you eat every day, but it is still made by much the same process. What did we have to do to make bread? *(Pantomime any appropriate actions that the children suggest.)*

C: Put on our aprons! Put on our hats! Wash our hands! Find the recipe! Sift the ingredients! Stir the mixture! Knead the dough! Shape the loaf! Bake the bread! Eat the bread!

L: Bread making takes time, but we enjoy the results. God took time to prepare the world for the birth of Jesus, the Bread of Life. Another group of people took time to find the promised Messiah. They traveled a long way from their countries in the East. Do you remember what we call them?

C: Wise men!

L: That's right! Today we are celebrating the special season that comes after Advent and Christmas, called Epiphany. Epiphany is a word that means "the revelation of Jesus as the Christ." Epiphany is the "Aha!" moment in the church year. When the wise men visited Jesus, they bowed in reverence even though they were kings themselves. That's because they recognized Jesus as God's gift of salvation for the world. God sent Jesus as the Bread of Life to Bethlehem, the "house of bread," so that people need not be spiritually hungry. All people around the world get hungry and need bread to eat every day, but all people also need God's presence in their lives every day. Aha! On Epiphany, we remember that God's gift is to the whole world, not only to those exactly like us. As we share these different breads, we can celebrate the message of Epiphany that Jesus is the Savior for the whole world. Let's take time to remember our world in prayer before we share our Epiphany breads.

Dear God *(pause for echo)*, thank you for sending Jesus *(pause)*, so that the whole world may be fed by your love *(pause)*. Amen. *(Share the variety of breads with the children.)*

Ann Liechty and Phyllis Wezeman

Contributors

Brant D. Baker holds graduate degrees from Princeton Theological Seminary and Columbia Theological Seminary. He served churches in the southern United States prior to becoming senior pastor of First Presbyterian Church in Mesa, Arizona. Dr. Baker has written numerous books, including three on children's sermons. He has been the editor of the *Abingdon Children's Sermon Library* since its inception. Brant is married and has two teenage children.

Karen Evans is the Minister of Spiritual Formation and Family Ministries at First United Methodist Church in Pensacola, Florida, where she has served for nineteen years. Karen is a graduate of Huntingdon College and Duke Divinity School. She also has a specialist degree in Education from the University of Florida. Karen is an ordained deacon in The United Methodist Church, a certified Christian educator, and a spiritual director. Karen is married and has two teenage children. Her passions include children and youth, stories, Duke basketball, and walking the spiritual journey with others.

Lisa Flinn delights in walking in the woods with her dog, year-round gardening with husband Bill, laughing with "The Ladies," the latest creations done by artsy children, playing with the grand-girls, and "striving side by side for the faith" at Hillsborough Presbyterian Church. She and co-author, Barbara Younger, have been writing for churches and children for twenty years. Their most recent books from Abingdon Press are: *Mystery in the Stable, Unwrapping the Christmas Crèche,* and *Celebrating God's World in Children's Church.*

Heather Hagler received a master's degree in Christian Education from Asbury Theological Seminary. She serves the Lord as a preschool teacher, a freelance writer, wife to Ken (a United Methodist pastor and church planter), and mother of two children, Logan and Jillian. To relax she likes to write, read, spend time with her family, and hike in the north Georgia mountains near her home.

Delia Halverson is an internationally known Christian education consultant, workshop leader, and keynote speaker. She has authored twenty books including: *The Nuts and Bolts of Christian Education, 32 Ways to Become a Great Sunday School Teacher, Side by Side: Families Learning and Living in Faith Together,* and *Growing the Soul: Meditations from My Garden.* Delia and her husband have lived all across the United States, and currently reside in Florida.

Randy Hammer is pastor of First Congregational Church, United Church of Christ, of Albany, New York. He holds an MDiv from Memphis Theological Seminary and a DMin from Meadville Lombard Theological School. His other published works include: *Dancing in the Dark: Lessons in Facing Life's Challenges with Courage and Creativity* (Pilgrim Press), and *Everyone a Butterfly: Forty Sermons for Children* (Skinner House).

Jeff L. Hutcheson is pastor of the First Presbyterian Church of Cleveland, Georgia. He has also served congregations in Florida and Alabama. Jeff received a Master of Divinity from Columbia Theological Seminary, and also holds a Master in Psychology from Auburn University at Montgomery, Alabama. He continues to be an aspiring writer and is currently completing a PhD in Human and Organizational Development. He lives in the "gateway to the mountains" with his wife and their two dogs, Chewy and Gizmo.

Susan M. Lang is a church consultant and pastor in the Evangelical Lutheran Church in America. She is the author of several books, including: *Our Community: Dealing with Conflict in Our Congregation* (Augsburg Fortress, 2002), and *Welcome Forward: A Field Guide for Global Travelers,* co-authored with Rochelle Melander (ELCA, 2005).

She publishes the *RevWriter Resource*, a free electronic newsletter for busy church leaders (www.revwriter.com).

Ann Liechty is a National Board Certified teacher and chair of the English Department at Plymouth High School in Indiana. She has worked as a religious education volunteer, teacher, consultant, and youth programming director. She has consulted with congregations about their educational ministry, and has written a wide variety of religious education materials. Ann lives in Plymouth, Indiana with her husband, Ron, a retired pastor. They have five children, ten grandchildren, and a great-grandson.

William Robert (Bob) Sharman III, a Presbyterian minister, has served churches in Alabama, and in Germany where he served the American Protestant Church of Bonn. He presently serves as senior minister at Jamestown Presbyterian Church in Jamestown, North Carolina. A graduate of the University of Mississippi, Princeton Theological Seminary, and Columbia Theological Seminary, Dr. Sharman is committed to excellence in children's sermons. He is married, has three children and a golden retriever, and believes it is a terrific practice to rehearse children's sermons with your pet!

Phyllis Wezeman is president of Active Learning Associates, Inc., and director of Christian Nurture at First Presbyterian Church in South Bend, Indiana. Phyllis has served as adjunct faculty in education in various settings, and has taught in Russia and China. She holds an MS in Education from Indiana University, is a recipient of three Distinguished Alumni Awards, and is widely published. Phyllis and her husband, Ken, have three children and three grandsons.

Barbara Younger, along with her friend Lisa Flinn, is the author of over fifteen books for Abingdon Press including *Mystery in the Stable, Unwrapping the Christmas Creche*, and *Celebrating God's World in Children's Church*. She is presently studying for an MFA in Writing for Children and Young Adults. Barbara has two grown daughters, and lives in Hillborough, North Carolina, with her husband, Cliff, and her cat, Lillian.

Scripture Index